Gogol's

The Government Inspector

Michael Beresford

Bristol Classical Press

Critical Studies in Russian Literature

First published in 1997 by
Bristol Classical Press
an imprint of
Gerald Duckworth & Co. Ltd
61 Frith Street
London W1D 3JL
e-mail: inquiries@duckworth-publishers.co.uk
Website: www.ducknet.co.uk

Reprinted 2001

A catalogue record for this book is available
from the British Library

ISBN 1-85399-439-1

Acknowledgement
The author is grateful to the editors of the Edwin Mellen Press
for permission to use material from his book, *N.V. Gogol, Peвизор*
(The Government Inspector), A Comedy in Five Acts (1996).

Printed in Great Britain by
Antony Rowe Ltd, Eastbourne

Contents

Introduction

The Government Inspector, a work of enormous comic power, with penetrating shafts of satire and a gallery of unforgettable characters, is the greatest play in the Russian language and one of the acknowledged masterpieces of world drama.

Probably no other play has had such a long, complex history of misunderstandings and misinterpretations. Gogol maintained that his purpose in writing it was to exert a moral influence on corrupt officials. Convinced of the redemptive power of art, he believed he could move public servants to mend their ways by exposing them to ridicule on the stage. His comedy, first presented in 1836, was laughed off by many of his contemporaries as an improbable farce, and most of them saw it, erroneously, as an implicit attack on the whole tsarist system.

Gogol's reforming purpose was not fulfilled but his drama, because of its universal theme of human corruption and its artistic excellence as much as the denunciatory significance attached to it, outlived its own time to become firmly established as a literary classic and as the leading play in the Russian dramatic repertoire. Outside Russia, too, it has acquired lasting popularity through its numerous translations and adaptations. It continues to amuse and delight audiences in many parts of the world, and to challenge the skill of producers and actors alike, offering great scope for diverse kinds of treatment.

In *The Government Inspector* Gogol departed from the tradition of comedy that had grown up in Russia from the eighteenth century. He retained the structure and many of the technical devices of conventional comedy, but purged it of much of its artificiality and extended its range, freeing it from the limitations of the love-plot with a happy ending. There is no trace in Gogol's play of the didacticism that characterises earlier Russian comedies. There are no champions of virtue, no knights in shining moral armour. His characters, unlike those of his predecessors, are not neatly divided into good and bad, but are living people who, though mostly rogues, all display a mixture of qualities, some good, some bad. His comedy, both in its characterisation and in its language, is much nearer to real life than any previous Russian play. He thus gave to Russian drama a new orientation, preparing the ground for later playwrights, such as Ostrovsky, Chekhov and Gorky.

The Plot

The plot of *The Government Inspector* is simple and unoriginal. Khlestakov, a vain, feather-brained young man who works in the capital, St. Petersburg, is returning to his father's country estate when, having lost all his money gambling at cards, he becomes stranded in a small provincial town. He is taken by the local officials to be a government inspector who, they are led to believe, is travelling incognito in their province. Finding himself fawned upon and treated as an important personage, Khlestakov begins to live up to the part and after being wined and dined he indulges in extravagant lies and shameless fanfaronade, making himself out to be a grand Petersburg celebrity who is both a highly respected official and a prolific man of letters. He exploits the situation with relish, accepting gifts and money offered to him as bribes. In rapid succession he woos the Governor's daughter and wife, becomes engaged to the former, then abruptly departs. Shortly afterwards the townspeople discover his true identity from a letter, opened by the local postmaster, in which Khlestakov makes most unflattering remarks about all the officials. Before they have time to recover from their shocked sense of outrage they are plunged into consternation by the announcement that the real inspector has arrived.

This comedy plot, based on the age-old theatrical device of mistaken identity, was transformed by Gogol's literary genius into a consummate work of drama. *The Government Inspector* is an indictment of dishonest officials not only in tsarist Russia but everywhere, at all times, and its satire goes beyond the sphere of bribery and corruption, striking at the vulgarity, triviality and philistinism found in many human beings. First and foremost, however, it is a brilliant, amusing exposure of the jobbery and skulduggery practised by Russian bureaucrats in the time of Nicholas I. It is only in the context of this historical period that the play can be fully understood and appreciated.

Part One

1. Historical Background

The reign of Nicholas I (1825-55) began with the Decembrist Revolt, in which a group of noblemen, most of them serving in the army, tried to seize the reins of power. The rebellion of 14 December[1] was swiftly crushed and the insurgents, after a lengthy investigation, were severely punished. The leading conspirators were hanged and most of the others were either banished to Siberia or condemned to serve in the ranks in remote parts of the empire. This attempted coup d'état left an indelible impression on Nicholas, who dedicated himself to defend the established order by imposing the strictest discipline on his realm. Fearing treason and subversion, he ruled Russia for thirty years with a rod of iron, introducing repressive measures and multiplying the agencies of inspection in every sphere of life.

The Tsar, a stern, majestic figure, dominated his country. He was trained as a soldier and possessed the soul of a martinet. He nearly always wore military uniform in public, was frequently present at parades and reviews, and drilled his Household Guards in person. He gave preference to army men over civilians and demanded unquestioning obedience from all his subjects. Under him the Russian people were regimented and their country, in the words of one contemporary, resembled a huge barracks. Punishments were generally inflicted with great harshness and cruelty. Common criminals had the Russian letters В-О-Р stamped on their faces with branding-irons[2] and soldiers often died after being made to run the gauntlet several times through lines of hundreds of men. So widespread was the practice of beating subordinates that the Tsar earned the popular nickname of 'Nicholas the Rod' (Николай Палкин). In foreign affairs he became the head of the ultra-conservative powers in Europe, allying himself with the monarchs of Austria and Prussia. He maintained a large standing army which was used to suppress rebellion both at home and abroad. His soldiers quelled the Polish uprising of 1830-1 and brought Hungary back into submission to the Austrian crown in 1849, so that Russia came to acquire the reputation of being 'the gendarme of Europe'.

Compared with the states of Western Europe, Russia was a backward country. Its economy, almost entirely agrarian, was beset with difficulties, including inadequate means of transport, a shortage of capital, a scarcity of skilled labour, and the extremely low purchasing power of the masses. The chief obstacle to progress was the fact that more than three-quarters of the population were peasants belonging either to the state or, as serfs, to the landowning gentry, who treated them as chattels. For quite minor offences male serfs could be flogged, deported to Siberia or sent into the army by their masters. Even the Tsar realised the iniquity of this system and disapproved of it, but feared the consequences of abolishing it at a stroke. In 1842 he observed at a meeting of the Council of State: 'There is no doubt that serfdom, as it exists in our country today, is an evil palpable and obvious to everyone, but to touch it *at present* would be even more disastrous'. In the same year he declared that the land belonged in perpetuity to the landowners and that he would never grant the serfs freedom. There was, it is true, some improvement in the lot of the peasantry during his reign, inasmuch as some of the worst abuses of the serf system were removed. Landowners were forbidden to sell serfs without land as a means of settling private debts, or to sell them by public auction, so as not to split peasant families. Serfs whose owners had gone bankrupt were given the right to buy their liberty. State peasants were given larger plots of land and provided with some welfare facilities, such as schools and a medical service. But these reforms, owing to the malpractices of local bureaucrats, were not put into full effect and thus did little to improve the condition of most peasants. Discontent was rife among them and there was a steady increase in the number of incidents in which manor-houses were burnt down and landlords, together with their bailiffs, assaulted or murdered. Such outbreaks of violence were put down by the military with great cruelty.

The administrative machine of the Russian Empire under Nicholas was based on the system instituted by Peter the Great and later modified by Catherine II. Both central and local organs of government were run by officials, who were appointed by the authorities and graded according to a hierarchy of ranks corresponding to those in the army. The holder of each rank had his own privileges, bore a special title, and was required to wear uniform when on duty. Promotion was much sought after, as was the prestige attaching to membership of various honorary orders, each with its own insignia and ceremonial. The civil service was staffed by members of the gentry, who were organised at local level into their own corporations and allowed to elect certain officials from among their number. In the provinces town councils were elected on the basis of a restricted franchise and in practice they became bodies of merchants whose scope of action was severely circumscribed. Real power lay with the police and other officials, who were responsible not to the local population but to the governor of the province and ultimately to the authorities in St. Petersburg. Under Nicholas this administrative organisation remained substantially unchanged, despite the fact that a special committee spent several years studying it and produced various proposals for reform.

The outstanding feature of Nicholas's regime was the centralisation of the state apparatus, accompanied by a great increase in bureaucracy. The

Tsar, a firm believer in autocracy, kept as much political power as possible in his own hands. He considered that the tasks of government, especially policy decisions, were for him alone, not for the Council of State or the Senate, still less for the Committee of Ministers. Accordingly, a fundamental change was made in the machinery of central government – the most significant change in the entire reign of Nicholas. In 1826 the Imperial Chancellery, which had been relatively unimportant until that time, was transformed into a key organ of state and expanded into several sections, each of which acted independently and was answerable only to the Tsar.

The First Section continued the original function of the Chancellery, dealing with court matters, the appointment and supervision of senior officials, and the management of the crown estates. The Second Section undertook the formidable task of compiling and codifying all existing laws, a genuine achievement in the sphere of jurisprudence. The administration of law, however, remained deplorably slow and cumbersome. All cases were heard *in camera*, with the proceedings conducted entirely in writing. Litigation dragged on interminably and arrested persons were often held in custody for years before their cases were tried.

The Third Section, together with the Corps of Gendarmes, a special armed police force formed at the same time, constituted the real centre of political power. Its functions included the collecting of information relating to state security, the surveillance of all politically suspect persons, religious dissidents and foreigners, the supervision of prisons and places of exile, and the eradication of corrupt practices in administration. It rapidly grew into a powerful intelligence organisation controlling a vast network of spies, agents and informers. So wide-ranging were its powers that it became a state within the state. It was independent of ordinary legal procedures and frequently acted as a judicial body with powers to detain and punish. People were arbitrarily arrested and beaten for quite minor offences, and their correspondence was opened and perused. Absolute secrecy prevailed in all branches of administration and fear of inspection or denunciation became widespread, although Russian officials were traditionally well practised in the art of concealing the true state of affairs from their superiors and from inquisitive foreigners. The Marquis de Custine, a Frenchman who visited Russia in 1839, described it as a country of mutes in which fear replaced, or rather paralysed thought. 'The Tsar,' he wrote, 'is the only man in the empire to whom one can speak without fear of informers.'

Despite the numerous agencies of supervision and inspection it proved impossible to exercise effective control over all the outposts of administration, owing to the enormous size of the empire and its grossly inadequate system of communications. Bribery and extortion, which had become deeply entrenched in all departments of the administration, both civil and military, continued to thrive. In 1827 General Benkendorf, Head of the Third Section, received a report from his second in command, M. von Vock,

in which officials were castigated as the most corrupt element in society.
'Among them honest men are rarely to be found. Plunder, fraud, and
perverse interpretation of the laws – these are their trade.' A similar picture
of this period is given by the anonymous author of a political document
which circulated secretly at the time of the Crimean War. 'The letter of the
law was observed, but negligence and crime were allowed to go unpunished.
While grovelling in the dust before ministers and directors of departments,
in the hope of receiving *tchins*[3] and decorations, the officials stole unblush-
ingly; and theft became so common that he who stole the most was the most
respected.'[4] Some officials, to be sure, were honest and conscientious, but
most of them tyrannised over the local population, extracting bribes and
gifts in order to line their own pockets. No petitioner would appear empty-
handed, and if he was too poor to offer money he would present a cake, a
pot of honey, a towel or some other inducement. The venality that prevailed
in the dispensation of justice found expression in the popular saying: 'If you
have a hundred roubles the law is on your side' (Сто рублей есть, так и
правда твоя).

The administration of the Russian Empire was thus both corrupt and
incompetent. An important cause of corruption among officials was the fact
that all of them, save the highest, were miserably underpaid. The real value
of their salaries had declined owing to severe inflation, especially during
the Napoleonic wars, and was not restored even when increases were
granted by Nicholas in the mid-1830s. Administrative incompetence, on the
other hand, was largely the consequence of Russia's backwardness, for its
standards of education and professional training were considerably lower
than those in Western countries. Many of the landed gentry, after generations of property division by equal inheritance, had fallen on hard times, so
much so that by 1836 two-thirds of all their estates were mortgaged to the
government. As a result more and more of their sons moved into the towns
to take up official posts which offered the prospect of supplementing a low
income by taking bribes and of tasting the fashionable pleasures of urban
life. The ranks of the bureaucracy, except in the top posts, were filled with
men of poor education, which prevented Russia from developing a reliable,
efficient civil service. The country was governed by an army of remote,
anonymous functionaries operating a rigid, formalistic system of administration in which precedent and routine were paramount. In the capital, St.
Petersburg, there was a complex of offices that flooded the country with
orders, decrees and circulars. The whole of this immense empire was
strangled by red tape, cramped by administrative fetters, and oppressed by
a monstrous tyranny of paper over people.

In the field of education the Russian government sought to impose strict
discipline and a pattern of conformity in behaviour and thought. A law of
1828 extended the period of compulsory schooling and confirmed the

existing system of public education, at the same time defining the social composition of each type of school. In principle, parish schools were to be attended by children belonging to the lowest social classes, chiefly the peasantry, district schools were intended for children of petty officials, merchants and artisans, while high schools (гимназии) and universities were reserved almost exclusively for children of the gentry. By laws enacted in 1835 all forms of state education were brought under the direction of regional overseers, and strict supervision was introduced over discipline in both schools and universities. Religious instruction was made compulsory for students as well as schoolchildren. Universities, whose teachers were already regarded as state officials, lost nearly all their autonomy, since the Minister of Education was given the power to make appointments without consulting the academic boards. Further restrictions were imposed by introducing tuition fees in universities in 1839, and then raising the fees at both high schools and universities twice in the following decade. Finally, after 1848 university curricula were curtailed. The teaching of philosophy was restricted to courses in logic and psychology, which were handed over to the clergy, and courses in constitutional law were abolished altogether.

Education under Nicholas I was pursued in the spirit of 'official nationality', a doctrine first formulated in 1832 by Sergei Uvarov, shortly before he became Minister of Education. According to Uvarov, the only way to counteract the influence of West European ideas was to establish an educational system based on 'the truly Russian conservative principles of *Orthodoxy, autocracy and nationality,* which are our ultimate sheet-anchor and the surest guarantee of our country's strength and greatness'. Autocracy was the most important element in this triple formula, as the Tsar exercised supremacy over the Orthodox Church, and 'nationality', or rather 'national spirit' (народность), was taken in practice to mean unconditional loyalty to throne and altar. This doctrine, inculcated in all educational establishments, even found its literary apologists in Nikolai Grech and Faddei Bulgarin, two writers who were connected with the Third Section and jointly edited the journal *A Son of the Fatherland* and later the daily newspaper *The Northern Bee.*

The small minority of educated upper-class Russians suffered from the increasingly harsh measures imposed by the authorities. Travel abroad was made more and more difficult and finally stopped altogether. Nicholas, deeply suspicious of liberalism and freethinking, tightened the controls over all kinds of literature in an attempt to prevent the spread of subversive ideas. Foreign publications were admitted into the country only after the most rigorous examination, and the possession of a forbidden book was considered a grave offence, punishable with exile. A statute on censorship, issued in 1826, prohibited the publication of any matter that was deemed to disparage the monarchy or the church or which criticised, even indirectly, the existing order of society. Works of logic and philosophy, other than textbooks, were not to be published. Under a slightly more lenient decree, enacted in 1828, censors were relieved of the responsibility for guiding public opinion and correcting 'mistakes' of fact, and even style, in works submitted for publication.

The censorship system operated through a multiplicity of agencies. The general censorship was administered by boards nominally supervised by the Ministry of Education, but in practice largely dominated by the Third Section. In addition powers of censorship were exercised by each government ministry and at times by the Tsar himself. In 1837 a system of dual control was instituted, which required that each work should be examined by two censors. And when in 1848 a secret committee headed by Count D. Buturlin, the so-called 'censorship of the censors', went into operation almost every word of print was subjected to the closest scrutiny. The writer A.V. Nikitenko, himself a censor, observed in 1850 that 'if one counts all the persons in charge of censorship they will exceed the number of books printed in a year'.

Editors of literary journals were constantly harried and hounded. They required special permission to publish their periodicals, which could be closed down for giving offence to the authorities. Several journals were so banned and their editors either exiled or barred for a time from practising their profession. Thus in 1836, the year in which *The Government Inspector* first appeared, the journal *Telescope* was suppressed because its editor had published a *Philosophical Letter* in which the author, Petr Chaadayev, expressed the view that Russia was an intellectually barren country which had made no contribution to civilisation and that she should draw closer to Western Europe. The editor of *Telescope* was sent into exile, the censor who passed the article was dismissed, and the unfortunate Chaadayev, officially declared insane, was placed under medical observation.

The intelligentsia emerging in the 1830s became passionately concerned with Russia's national identity and historical destiny. Chaadayev's famous 'Letter' gave rise to a protracted dispute between the Westernisers, who believed that Russia should adopt West European culture and institutions, and the Slavophils, who held that Russia was a country apart, which should continue to cultivate its own native traditions. For all their differences of outlook, however, the men of both ideological camps were united in their detestation of the regime and opposition to the system of serfdom. They also shared a desire to be given freedom of speech and publication. But there was no freedom of expression in Russia and the discussion of ideas, which could not take place openly, was conducted through the medium of imaginative literature. In this way literature came more and more to reflect Russia's social problems and was turned into a weapon in the struggle for enlightenment and progress.

Writers naturally had to use great caution and often resorted to subterfuge, employing the so-called 'Aesopian language' of hints, allusions and circumlocutions in order to disguise their ideas. At the same time works which had been banned by the censors were freely circulated in manuscript copies. Thus, despite the shackles of censorship, literature flourished under Nicholas I. Indeed by a curious paradox of history his reign, which was one of reaction and stagnation in most spheres of life, produced a great ferment of ideas and a remarkable burgeoning of literary talent. Pushkin, Gogol and Lermontov were all at the height of their creative powers in the 1830s and in the latter part of the reign Turgenev, Dostoyevsky and Tolstoy made their literary debut. Of these great writers none was endowed with such fertile creative powers or displayed such extraordinary originality in the use of language as Gogol, one of the most complex and elusive figures in all Russian literature.

2. Productions and Criticisms

The theme of the stranger mistaken for an investigating official, on which the plot of *The Government Inspector* is based, was by no means fanciful or far-fetched, given the conditions prevailing in the empire of Nicholas I. Contemporary records mention several authentic cases of visitors to the Russian provinces being taken for inspectors from the capital and received with great deference by the local officials, who had good reason to fear the long arm of the authorities in St. Petersburg. Nor was the theme a new one in literature. The German dramatist August von Kotzebue, whose plays were very popular in Russia, where he lived for several years, treated the subject of the impostor in his satirical comedy *Die deutschen Kleinstädter* (1803), and the same theme was used, although without any satirical purpose, in A.F. Veltman's tale *The Provincial Actors* (1835). But the closest parallel to Gogol's plot is to be found in a didactic comedy, *The Visitor from the Capital*, by the Ukrainian writer Grigory Kvitka, who used the pen-name of Osnoviyanenko. This play, although not published until 1840, was written in 1827 and its plot is so strikingly similar to that of *The Government Inspector* in certain details that it seems reasonable to assume that Gogol at least knew of it and may even have read it in manuscript. However, none of these works is mentioned by Gogol as a source of inspiration and whatever thematic elements they have in common with his play, they are artistically almost as far removed from it as Holinshed's *Chronicles* are from Shakespeare's historical dramas.

In his *Author's Confession*, written in 1847, Gogol states that he was indebted to Pushkin for his plot, and this is corroborated by several of his contemporaries, including the critic and literary historian Pavel Annenkov. Count Vladimir Sollogub, a writer who knew Gogol for many years, states in his memoirs that the plot of *The Government Inspector* was based on two incidents recounted by Pushkin, who is said to have called himself the 'godfather' of the play. The first anecdote concerned a gentleman who visited the town of Ustyuzhna in Novgorod province, where he passed himself off as a ministry official and fleeced the local inhabitants. The second incident involved Pushkin himself, when he was visiting Orenburg province in the summer of 1833 to collect material for his *History of the Pugachev Rebellion*. At Nizhny Novgorod he dined with the governor of the province, M.P. Buturlin, who received him most courteously but found some of his enquiries rather disquieting. From there Pushkin went to the fortress town of Orenburg, where he stayed with the military governor, V.A. Perovsky, an old friend of his. One morning a letter from Buturlin arrived, warning the count to be on his guard with Pushkin, whom the writer suspected of being an inspector in disguise. Perovsky roared with laughter on reading the letter and showed it to the poet, who was quick to share his amusement.[5]

A quite different story is given by O.M. Bodyansky, Professor of Slavonic Studies at Moscow University, who was a friend of Gogol for many years. In his diary Bodyansky states that Gogol told him, during an evening at the Aksakovs in the autumn of 1851, that Pushkin supplied the original idea for the play. The poet had recounted how in the 1820s Pavel Svinyin, a prominent journalist, posed in Bessarabia as an important official from St. Petersburg and even began to accept petitions from prisoners before he was exposed as an impostor. Gogol added that he had heard subsequently of several similar escapades, one of them involving a man named Volkov.[6]

Apparently Pushkin himself intended at one time to write a tale or play on the theme of mistaken identity. The brief outline of his plot, written on paper bearing the watermark 1832, came to light only three-quarters of a century after his death. It reads as follows: '(Svinyin: *deleted*) Crispin arrives in the Province (NB for the fair) – he is taken for an Ambas[sador]. The Govern[or] is a worthy fool – the Gov[ernor's wife] flirts with him – Crispin asks for the daughter's hand.'[7] Pushkin may well have decided that the theme was better suited to Gogol's talents than his own and gratuitously presented it to him. It is possible, however, that Gogol simply appropriated the theme from Pushkin, judging from a remark the latter is reported to have made in reference to *The Government Inspector* and *Dead Souls*. According to Annenkov, Pushkin did not give Gogol these subjects entirely of his own free will and laughingly observed to some of his intimates: 'One has to be very wary with this Ukrainian; he robs me before I have time to shout for help.'

It is not known which of the several anecdotes Gogol used for his play, nor is it possible to say exactly when he heard them from Pushkin, although clearly it must have been some time during the period 1833-35. In most modern editions of Gogol's work it is stated that *The Government Inspector* was written following a request made in a letter to Pushkin which Gogol wrote from St. Petersburg on 7 October 1835. 'Do me a favour,' he asked, 'give me some plot, it doesn't matter whether it is amusing or not, so long as it is a purely Russian anecdote. Meanwhile my hand is trembling to write a comedy... Do please give me a plot; I'll produce a five-act comedy in one burst and I swear it will be funnier than the devil!' No reply to this letter exists, and since Pushkin did not return from his country estate to St. Petersburg until 23 October he could not have answered Gogol's request verbally much before the end of that month. And we know (from a letter

Gogol wrote to Pogodin) that the play was finished on 4 December. 'I have been so preoccupied all this time,' he wrote two days later, 'that I only just managed to finish the play the day before yesterday.'

From the evidence of these two letters it is generally assumed that the play, at least in its original version, was written between the end of October and 4 December 1835, that is in just over a month. There are grounds for suspecting, however, that Gogol may have begun to write the play before October 1835, as his earlier biographers believed. One of them, V.I. Shenrok, reports a story told to him in 1884 by Alexander Danilevsky, who was then seventy-five. The old man recalled that when they were once travelling from Kiev to Moscow with Ivan Pashchenko, another old schoolfellow, Gogol staged a real-life rehearsal of *The Government Inspector*, 'on which he was then working intensively'. He sent Pashchenko ahead to announce at all the post-stations that an inspector was on his way, travelling incognito. The stratagem worked perfectly. Gogol, whose travel document showed him to be an associate professor (адъюнкт-профессор), was taken by most of the postmasters to be someone scarcely less exalted than an aide-de-camp (адъютант) to the Tsar. He asked various seemingly innocent questions and was treated with exceptional courtesy, being given fresh horses without delay. The journey proceeded very smoothly, a most unusual thing in Russia at that time.[8]

If Danilevsky's story was true, this incident could only have occurred in August 1835 while Gogol was still a university professor and when, as we know from other sources, he did in fact travel from Kiev to Moscow. This conflicting evidence makes it impossible to determine exactly when Gogol began his play, but the first draft cannot have been started much before the beginning of 1835, since it contains a reference to Meyerbeer's opera *Robert le Diable*, which was first performed in St. Petersburg in December 1834.

Soon after *The Government Inspector* was completed Gogol tried it out on a private audience, as he did with many of his writings. On 18 January 1836 he read the play before a literary gathering at the home of the poet Zhukovsky and it was acclaimed with enthusiasm, especially by Pushkin, who laughed uproariously. Only one person failed to share the general amusement, namely Baron Yegor Rozen, a prolific but mediocre writer who thought himself a great dramatist and regarded Gogol as a mere caricaturist. Prince P.Vyazemsky, an eminent poet and critic who was present at the reading, doubted whether the play would be as successful on the stage since few actors would be able to match Gogol's masterly solo performance of his own work.

Contemporary accounts vary as to how the play reached the stage, but Gogol was certainly fortunate in having influential friends to help him in the difficult task of obtaining approval from the censors. Only a few years earlier, in 1828, a new system of censorship had been introduced, whereby playwrights were required to submit their works to the ordinary censor for publication and to the Third Section for permission to have them performed. Whether Gogol submitted his play to the censors immediately is not certain. A.I. Wolf, a theatre historian, states that Gogol sent the text of his play to the ordinary censors, who were so alarmed at its contents that they flatly refused to pass it for publication.[9] As there is no contemporary evidence to support this, however, it is quite possible that Gogol tried to circumvent the censorship in the first instance. At all events he decided to appeal through his friends to the supreme censor, the Tsar himself.

According to Wolf's account Zhukovsky, supported by Vyazemsky and a wealthy courtier, Count Mikhail Vielgorsky, interceded on Gogol's behalf and succeeded in obtaining royal patronage for the play. A different and generally discredited account of all this is given by Alexandra Smirnova, a celebrated court beauty, who states in her memoirs that Gogol read his play at one of her soirées and that Pushkin asked her to use her influence with the Tsar to secure its approval for performance on the stage.[10] Whether the Tsar read the play in manuscript, as Vyazemsky states, or whether it was read aloud to him at court, as Wolf maintains, in either case it found favour with the Emperor, who authorised its public performance. On 27 February a copy of the manuscript reached the censor of the Third Section, E.Oldekop, who deemed it suitable for the stage. In his lengthy report, written in French, Oldekop described the play as witty and excellently written, and after summarising its plot he pronounced that it contained nothing objectionable. The only important change he made was to exclude the N.C.O.'s wife from the second petitioning scene in Act IV, although, curiously enough, two of the Governor's allusions to her flogging were left uncensored. A number of minor textual alterations and deletions were made on moral or religious grounds. Thus, in Act V Khlestakov was not allowed to boast, in his letter to Tryapichkin, that he intended to cuckold the Governor, and the latter's revelation that he had lied to a priest at confession was suppressed. A few invocations to God and the saints of the church were allowed to stand, but many were modified or removed so as not to offend pious feelings. For example, the interjection ей-богу ('I swear to God') was frequently toned down to ей-ей ('I swear') or deleted altogether. Similarly, the Governor's ejaculation Батюшки, сватушки! Выносите, святые угодники! ('Holy fathers! Saints of heaven preserve us!') was replaced by the feebler Ай-ай-ай! ('Oh dear! Oh dear!').[11]

Acting on Oldekop's report General Dubbelt, a senior official in the Third Section, granted permission on 2 March for the play to be performed. Soon after this, on 13 March, the play, with substantially the same changes, was approved for publication by the censor A.V. Nikitenko. Meanwhile, with the Tsar's prior assent, rehearsals had already begun towards the end of February at the Alexandrinsky Theatre, the finest playhouse in St. Petersburg.[12] The production was under the general supervision of Alexander Khrapovitsky, a bureaucrat quite devoid of any artistic sense. The author, following a common theatrical practice of the time, took an active part in the rehearsals, acting as co-producer. Gogol, who made alterations in the stage text until a few days before the play opened, was present in the theatre giving advice on decor, costume and the interpretation of roles, most of which went unheeded. Special sets were designed, something most unusual for a new production in those days. But Gogol insisted that the opulent furnishings provided for the opening scene should be replaced by something more modest. He also made the actor playing Osip change from livery resplendent with gold braid into a grimy old frock-coat.

The management refused Gogol's request for a dress rehearsal on the grounds that it was not customary and in any case was quite unnecessary, since the actors knew their job. Unfortunately, however, most of the actors, trained to perform highly stylised plays far removed from real life, were puzzled by this new kind of comedy. It conformed neither to the canons of neo-classical comedy nor to the type of vaudeville which dominated the Russian stage at that time. Petr Karatygin, a prolific vaudevillist and a member of the company, tells us that when Gogol first read his play to the actors they did not know what to make of it. '"What is this?" his listeners whispered to each other after the reading had finished. "Is it supposed to be a comedy? He certainly reads well, but what language he uses! The man-servant actually speaks like a servant and the locksmith's wife Poshlepkina is nothing but a common peasant woman taken straight from Haymarket Square...[13] What do Zhukovsky and Pushkin see in it?"'

Karatygin has left us a vivid description of Gogol at the final rehearsal. Some of the younger actors were evidently less amused by the play than by its author, who cut a strange, comical figure. 'Gogol was greatly agitated and obviously upset ... He was a short man with fair hair piled up enormously at the front, gold-rimmed spectacles perched on his long, beaky nose, screwed-up little eyes and tightly pursed lips... His green coat with long tails and tiny pearl buttons, his brown trousers and the tall top-hat which Gogol would now doff with a jerk, running his fingers through his topknot, then twirl around in his hands – all this made him look something of a caricature.'[14]

At the first performance of the play, given on 19 April 1836, the auditorium of the Alexandrinsky Theatre was packed with a glittering assembly. The stalls were occupied by nobles, men of letters and several ministers of state, while the gallery was filled with lesser mortals – junior officials, shopkeepers, students and others. Just before the curtain rose the Tsar appeared in the royal box, accompanied by the Crown Prince. Nicholas seems to have thoroughly enjoyed the spectacle. He laughed heartily and applauded several times during the performance, and his obedient ministers followed suit. On leaving his box he is said to have remarked to those near him: 'That was quite a play! Everyone has taken a knocking, myself most of all!'[15] Nicholas, who had an open contempt for the whole of his vast bureau-cracy and was well aware of the bribery and corruption that permeated it, was no doubt well pleased to see dishonest officials publicly pilloried. But he evidently did not foresee the social and political impact the play would make on educated audiences, otherwise he would certainly have banned it. In fact he commanded the rest of the royal family and his other ministers to go and see it, and made presents of money to three of the actors. Gogol himself was given 800 roubles as a mark of appreciation for presenting the Tsar with a copy of the play. He received a further 2,500 roubles from the director of the St. Petersburg theatres for the performing rights.

The most reliable and substantial account of the premiere is that given by Pavel Annenkov in his memoirs. 'Even after the first act everyone was looking puzzled (it was a select audience in the full sense of the word), as if no one knew what to make of what he had just seen. After this the bewilderment increased with each act. Most of the spectators, unaccustomed to expect this sort of thing in the theatre, were thrown off balance by it and seemed to take comfort in assuming that they were watching a farce, an opinion they clung to with unshakeable determination. Yet there were some features and scenes in this farce which rang so true that once or twice there was a burst of general laughter, especially in the parts that were least at variance with the conception of a comedy held by most of the spectators. Things took a different turn in the fourth act: laughter still echoed across the auditorium from time to time, but it was a rather timid laughter that died away in an instant. There was hardly any applause at all, but the rapt attention, the intense concentration with which the audience followed every subtlety of the action, and the dead silence that occasionally reigned, showed that they were passionately gripped by what was happening on the stage. By the end of the act the earlier bewilderment had turned into an almost unanimous feeling of indignation, which was brought to a climax by the fifth act. Many people called for the author at the end because he had written a real comedy, others because some of the scenes showed talent, and the ordinary spectators because the play had made them laugh. But the general opinion expressed on all sides amongst this select audience could be summed up in the words: "This is impossible, it's a slander and a farce".'[16]

Gogol, who shared a box with Zhukovsky, Vyazemsky and Vielgorsky, had arrived in the theatre with a deep sense of foreboding and he suffered agonies throughout the evening. He expressed his feelings on this occasion in 'a letter to a certain writer'. '*The Government Inspector* has been played,' he wrote, 'and I feel so down at heart,[17] so strange... I knew before it started how things would go, yet for all that a sad and disagreeable feeling of oppres-sion overcame me. My own work seemed repugnant and outlandish to me, as if it were not mine at all... From the very beginning of the performance I sat in the theatre feeling downcast. I was not worried about the audience's reaction or whether it would be enthusiastic. Of all those present in the house there was only one judge I feared, – and that was myself. Inwardly I could hear reproaches and grumbles about my play which drowned out everything else. However, the audience was pleased on the whole. Half of them even gave the play a sympathetic reception; the other half, as is usual, abused it, but for reasons which have nothing to do with art.'[18]

The author was well pleased with Sosnitsky, who acted the part of the Governor, and with Afanasiev, who played Osip, but found the rest of the players woefully inadequate. The celebrated vaudeville actor Dyur (Dure) had utterly failed to grasp the character of Khlestakov, whom he portrayed as a typical stage villain and calculating trickster, quite contrary to the sense of the text, which clearly shows that the hero does not set out deliberately to dupe or cheat the town officials. Gogol was also dissatisfied with most of the costumes, and simply gasped with horror at the ridiculous garb in which Bobchinsky and Dobchinsky were attired. These pot-bellied squires, who should be neat and well groomed, appeared untidy and dishevelled in very tall grey wigs, with enormous shirt-fronts sticking out of their breeches. Finally, the dumb scene at the end of the play was badly mismanaged. The curtain was rung down at the wrong moment, so that the play seemed to be left hanging in mid-air. Gogol blamed the theatre people for this failure, complaining bitterly that they would not listen to him. This scene, to which he attached great importance, could only succeed, he said, if it was presented as a *tableau vivant* in which each of the actors adopts a pose that reflects an individual reaction appropriate to the character he is portraying.

At the end of the performance Gogol left the theatre immediately, without taking a bow. He went to call on Pletnev, a literary acquaintance, who was not at home, and then visited his old schoolfellow, Nikolai Prokopovich, arriving at his house in an irritable mood. His host handed him a copy of the play, which had appeared in print that same day, with the words: 'Take an admiring look at your little son.' Gogol flung the book on the floor, went over to the table and leaning on it, said pensively: 'Lord! If just one or two people had abused it I wouldn't have cared, but everyone, everyone...'

Despite the fact that *The Government Inspector* was played in the style of a vaudeville, it made a great impact on the audiences and caused a great stir in the capital. Every performance was booked out in advance and the play provoked lively and sometimes heated controversy. In this sense it was a success. In Gogol's eyes, however, it was a failure, indeed a twofold disaster, because the actors, or most of them, had presented a complete travesty of his artistic intentions, and because his moral purpose had not been understood at all. The reception of the play by public and critics alike was a mixture of violent obloquy and enthusiastic praise. Some, like the popular playwright Kukolnik and the finance minister Kankrin, dismissed it as a cheap farce unworthy of serious consideration. At the same time many people saw in this 'farce', as it was then generally taken to be, an implicit denunciation of the whole social and political system of their country.

Liberals and progressives applauded Gogol's exposure of the vices of provincial officialdom as a bold, albeit indirect attack on those in power at the top. On the other hand, the conservatives and most of those in high official positions regarded it as an impudent, outrageous calumny against Russia and her government, a calculated attempt at subversion. This attitude was epitomised by Khrapovitsky in his diary entry on the evening of the premiere. 'The play is extremely amusing,' he noted, 'only there is intolerable abuse of the gentry, officials and merchants.' In short, few people saw in the play what Gogol had intended, namely a moral satire aimed at exposing and correcting the abuses practised by all but a mere handful of Russian officials.

The play was a great success with the majority of ordinary theatre-goers in St. Petersburg, and especially with the younger generation, but most of the members of high society were displeased or even scandalised by what they regarded as its vulgar tone and its subversive tenor. Writing to his friend Alexander Turgenev on 8 May, Prince Vyazemsky said: 'Everyone tries to be more of a monarchist than the Tsar, and they are all angry that permission was given to perform this play which was, nevertheless, a brilliant and total success on the stage, though not in the sense of winning universal approval. It is incredible what stupid opinions you hear about it, especially in the higher circles of society! "As if such a town existed in Russia." "How is it possible not to present on the stage a single honest, decent man? Are we to believe there are no such people in Russia?"' Typical of this kind of reaction was an indignant outburst by a prominent official, F.F. Vigel, who, before he had even seen or read the play, described it in a letter to the playwright Mikhail Zagoskin as a slander in five acts. 'The author,' he wrote, 'has created a fictitious Russia and a particular small town in which he has dumped all the loathsome things you occasionally find on the surface of the real Russia: what a heap of knavery, baseness and ignorance he has piled up ... I know this gentleman who is the author of *The Government Inspector* – he typifies young Russia with all its impudence and cynicism.'[19]

A similar attitude no doubt lay behind the refusal by members of the Academy of Sciences to award Gogol a gold medal for his play. The proposal to confer this distinction on him was made by Pavel Demidov, a wealthy manufacturer and patron of the arts who donated 25,000 roubles each year to be distributed in prizes by a special committee of the Academy. Demidov warmly commended Gogol to the committee for having graced Russian literature with a new work which 'may be regarded as a model of its kind in the depiction of characters'. At a plenary meeting of academicians held on 13 May the proposal was rejected on the grounds that the rules of the competition specifically excluded literary works. And when Demidov later asked that the clause in question should be deleted, his request was refused.[20]

The reviewers in the St. Petersburg press for the most part treated Gogol's play as a farce, at best amusing and at worst positively harmful. Petr Serebreny, writing in the literary supplement to *The Russian Invalid*,[21] described it as an innocent, light-hearted piece which would 'cure many a sorrow and banish many a depression'. Its harshest critics were Faddei Bulgarin and Osip Senkovsky, both of them zealous apologists for the government and dedicated literary enemies of Gogol. Bulgarin, in a long article which he published in two consecutive issues of his newspaper *The Northern Bee*,[22] said that Gogol was undoubtedly a talented writer and his play was vastly amusing, but it was no comedy, for a real comedy, he dogmatically asserted, could not be based on administrative malpractices. The play was no more than a hilarious farce on a hackneyed theme, with a plot that was both trivial and highly improbable. In his view Osip, Bobchinsky and Dobchinsky were masterly, life-like portrayals of character, but the rest of the *dramatis personae* seemed to him ludicrous caricatures lacking all human attributes except the gift of speech, which they employed to indulge in idle chatter. In no small town, and rarely even in large cities, would one find such flirts as Anna Andreyevna and her daughter – such coquetry was quite un-Russian. His moral sensibilities were offended by the spectacle of the two women treating Khlestakov as fair game and shamelessly squabbling about which of them he preferred. Such behaviour, commented the critic acidly, was just like that displayed by the savages of the Sandwich Islands when Captain Cook landed there.[23]

Bulgarin complained that the play provided no contrast between good and evil, but presented only rogues and fools. Moreover, the characters and customs shown in it bore no resemblance to anything in contemporary Russia but belonged to an age long past. 'It would be a great pity,' he remarked, 'if any of the spectators, unfamiliar with our provinces, thought that such morals and manners *really* existed in Russia or that there could be a town without a single honest soul in it...' Gogol's intention had been to describe a Russian district town, but in fact he had depicted a small town in the Ukraine or Belorussia. Finally, Bulgarin asserted that the play was larded with crudities of language such as he had never known on the Russian stage or in literature, and said it was unforgivable of Gogol to resort to the kind of coarse double entendres found in *The Government Inspector*. Bulgarin's general verdict on the play was that it made an unpleasant impression, for it offered 'no food for the mind or heart, neither ideas nor feelings'. In short, he considered that Gogol's comedy was devoid of social significance or artistic distinction and failed to reflect contemporary Russian reality.

Senkovsky, in his *Library for Reading*, published an unsigned review which contained substantially the same criticisms of the play as had been made by Bulgarin.[24] The reviewer approached the comedy somewhat differently, however, adopting an ostensibly sympathetic tone and showing himself eager to give helpful advice to the budding young dramatist. He acknowledged Gogol's exceptional comic gifts and commended several scenes in the play, quoting some of them at length, but warned its author to be on his guard against the excessive praise bestowed on him by some of his admirers.

The Government Inspector, albeit highly amusing, was a sordid drama which at times plumbed greater depths of vulgarity than the crudest of farces. Respect for his readers, the critic added, prevented him from quoting any of the offending passages. Though it showed promise for the future, the play had no literary merit and was devoid of any idea or message. It had no plot, he complained, meaning by this that it lacked the love interest which was an essential ingredient in traditional comedy, and he suggested that Gogol should remedy this defect by introducing a rival to Maria for Khlestakov's affections. Nor had the play any real characters, he observed, for the *dramatis personae* had been made to fit the requirements of the story. It was peopled throughout with scoundrels and fools whose actions were not inspired by human passions. Furthermore, the bad characters were not counterbalanced by any good ones, which was wholly at variance with what one found in real life.

Gogol's play, the reviewer claimed, was merely a dramatised version of a trite foreign anecdote told many times before in various languages, whereas a true comedy should treat the mores of a particular society (for him the word comedy was evidently synonymous with comedy of manners). 'Abuses cannot be the subject of a comedy,' he wrote, 'for they are not the morals of the people, nor are they characteristic of society as a whole but the crimes of a few individuals, and they should evoke in honest citizens indignation rather than laughter.' His patriotic sentiments were outraged by the way in which the play, while describing a local incident, purported to give a typical picture of the whole country. After admitting that corrupt practices existed among officials in remote provincial places, the critic concluded with the patently absurd objection that there was no reason to attribute them solely to Russia by transferring this international story to a Russian setting.

Two months later, after Gogol had left Russia, Vyazemsky refuted these criticisms point by point in a long article, which appeared in Pushkin's journal *The Contemporary*.[25] The play, in Vyazemsky's view, was a worthy successor to the satirical comedies of Fonvizin, Kapnist and Griboyedov. He defended the author's right to choose any subject he wished, however sordid or distasteful it might be, and pointed out that the language of the play, though vulgar and shocking at times to some ears, was entirely appropriate to the characters it presented. It was not a farce, he said, although there was an element of caricature in the portrayal. Its plot was perfectly credible, for similar cases of mistaken identity had been known to occur in actuality. The Governor's error concerning Khlestakov's identity, which Bulgarin had found a totally inconceivable blunder on his part, was quite understandable if one remembered the popular saying that 'fear has big eyes'.[26] The Governor and his fellow-officials learn of Khlestakov's arrival when they are in a state of panic. In this situation their mistake is entirely plausible.

Gogol's detractors had alleged that his play was immoral because it presented no virtuous characters and thus left out the better side of human nature. Vyazemsky objected that a work of literature could only be called immoral if it tended to corrupt people. But Gogol had merely presented immoral behaviour in a detached manner and shown only a part of life, not the whole of it. The comedy could not be said to slander Russia, for such people as those in the play existed in real life. All that Gogol had done was to assemble them in one imaginary place, using the artistic method of selection, in order to produce a typical, generalised picture. He was not in any way implying that there were no good people in Russia. In any case, the immorality of Gogol's characters should not be exaggerated, since they were 'more ridiculous than villainous' and displayed 'more ignorance and lack of education than depravity'. Nor was the plot of the play based on any criminal act or perversion of justice. 'It is said that there is not a single intelligent person in Gogol's comedy,' he concluded. 'This is not true – the author is intelligent. It is said that there is not a single honest and right-thinking person in Gogol's comedy. This is untrue: the honest and right-thinking person is the government which, while striking at abuses with all the force of the law, allows a writer of talent to correct them by using the weapon of ridicule.' For Vyazemsky, as for Gogol, *The Government Inspector* embodied not a political protest, but a moral indictment.

Gogol was not only distressed by the way his play was burlesqued on the stage, but also deeply perturbed by the public reaction to it. What alarmed him most was the political interpretation put on it – something he had not expected at all. He had hoped it would evoke a positive response and exert a beneficial influence on morals. Instead it had stirred up a violent controversy and brought down a storm of abuse from high officials and influential conservatives who considered it to be an attack on the whole system. He was equally embarrassed by the praise showered on it by liberals and progressives. He realised that he had badly miscalculated the effect his play would have and his correspondence at this time reflects his bitterness and disillusionment.[27]

In two letters to the historian Pogodin he complained, more in sorrow than in anger, about the way *The Government Inspector* had been so widely misinterpreted. On 10 May he wrote: 'I am not disturbed by the fact that positively every single class of society is now up in arms against me, but it is somehow distressing and sad to see your own countrymen, whom you love with all your heart, unjustly turned against you, to see how they pervert and misconstrue everything, taking the particular for the general and the exception for the rule. What is spoken truthfully and vividly actually seems to them a lampoon. Put two or three scoundrels on the stage and a thousand honest people say angrily: "We are not scoundrels"...It is time that I wrote with greater deliberation,' he concluded, clearly referring to the unfortunate misunderstandings his play had caused.

Five days later he took up the same theme again. 'It makes you sad,' he wrote, 'to see what a sorry plight the writer still finds himself in here in our country. Everyone is against him, and there is no countervailing force at all on his side. "He's an incendiary! He's a rebel!" And who says so? Men in high offices of state, men who have risen in the service, men of experience who should have sufficient intelligence to understand the true position, people who are considered to be educated and whom society, at least Russian society, calls educated – they are the ones who say this. Scoundrels appear on the stage and everyone is furious, demanding to know why they should appear. I don't mind scoundrels getting angry, but people I never took to be scoundrels are angry. I am saddened by this ignorant petulance, a sign of the profound, stubborn ignorance that pervades all classes of our society... Something that enlightened people would receive with loud laughter and sympathy provokes a splenetic outburst of ignorance, and this ignorance is found in everyone. If you call a crook a crook they consider you are undermining the foundations of the state; if you say something that is merely true to life it is interpreted as defaming a whole class of society and inciting its subordinates or others to turn against it.'

Meanwhile, preparations were in hand to present *The Government Inspector* in Moscow, but Gogol, who had originally intended to go there and help with the production, now changed his mind. He was so shaken and disheartened by the reception given to his play in St. Petersburg that he firmly resisted all efforts to persuade him to go to Moscow. On 29 April he sent a letter and several copies of the play to his friend Shchepkin, the distinguished actor who was to play a leading role in the Moscow production. In this letter he again voiced his strong feelings, which amounted almost to persecution mania. He persisted in believing, quite erroneously, that *everyone* was against him. 'Having made the acquaintance of the theatre managers here,' he wrote, 'I have become so disgusted with the theatre that the mere thought of the "pleasantness" in store for me at the Moscow theatre too is enough to deter me from making the trip to Moscow... Finally, to crown all the dirty tricks that could be possibly played on me, I understand the management here, that is to say the director Gedeonov, actuated by a petty personal dislike of some of the chief actors in my play, such as Sosnitsky and Dyur, has seen fit to give the main roles to other actors after four performances. It's all too much for me. Do what you like with my play, but I won't bother with it. I'm fed up with the play itself, as I am with all the fuss over it. The effect it had was to create a great furore. Everyone is against me. Elderly and respectable officials cry out, saying that nothing is sacred to me, daring to speak as I have done about civil servants. The police are against me, the merchants are against me, the literary men are against me...Now I realise what it means to be a comic writer. At the slightest whiff of truth they are up in arms against you – not just individuals, but whole classes of people.'

Gogol entrusted the Moscow production to Shchepkin, informing his friend that he had lost interest in the play and was dissatisfied with many things in it, though not the ones his critics had found fault with. When Shchepkin encountered resentment and lack of co-operation from his fellow-actors he asked Gogol to hand over the task of supervision, nominally at least, to his friend Sergei Aksakov. Gogol would agree to this only if it was absolutely necessary, still preferring Shchepkin to be in charge. In the end, however, the production was taken over by the playwright Mikhail Zagoskin, who was Director of the Moscow Theatres. It was mounted in a slapdash fashion after only about ten days of rehearsal, with little understanding and less enthusiasm on the part of Zagoskin, who was a literary rival of Gogol. New scenery was provided, but the costumes were antiquated and ridiculous. It was announced that the comedy would open at the Bolshoi Theatre on 24 May, but the management, fearing a public reaction similar to that in St. Petersburg, transferred it to the smaller Maly Theatre on the pretext that the Bolshoi was undergoing alterations.

The first performance in Moscow was given on 25 May to an audience composed, in the main, of people belonging to high society. Nearly all the actors at the Maly, like those at the Alexandrinsky Theatre, treated the play as a vaudeville and most of them failed to get under the skin of the characters they were playing. A few were successful in their parts, notably Potanchikov as the Postmaster, Stepanov as the Judge, Orlov as Osip, and above all Shchepkin, who made the Governor a more earthy, robust rogue than Sosnitsky had done. But Lensky, though superior to Dyur, was still a long way from interpreting the central role of Khlestakov as Gogol conceived it.

The play was given a cool reception by the predominantly aristocratic audience at this premiere and there were no curtain calls for any of the actors. The reaction of the spectators was described by Shchepkin in a letter he wrote to Sosnitsky on 3 June. 'The audience was amazed at its novelty,' he said, 'and roared with laughter a great deal, but I had expected it to get a much bigger reception. I was extremely surprised by this, but an acquaintance of mine gave me the following amusing explanation for it: "Come now," he said, "how could it have been better received when half the audience were bribees and the other half bribers?"'

After its first performance in Moscow the play was received with greater acclaim than in the capital and was a great success with the general public. In Moscow, as in St. Petersburg, it soon became the talk of the town and aroused violent hostility in some quarters. Sergei Aksakov tells us in his memoirs that the most malicious rumours were spread about Gogol in the highest official circles of Moscow and some even reached the ears of the Sovereign. Aksakov further states that Count Fedor Tolstoy, a prominent aristocrat, was heard to declare at a large private gathering that Gogol was 'an enemy of Russia who should be clapped in irons and sent to Siberia' and there were many people, especially in St. Petersburg, who were of the same opinion.[28]

The critical reviews of *The Government Inspector* published in Moscow were much more favourable than those which had appeared in the press of St. Petersburg. The first review was published in the journal *Moscow Observer* by its editor Vasily Androsov, a moderate Slavophil.[29] Androsov judged Gogol's comedy to be worthy of a high place among the few truly original dramatic works Russia had so far produced and described it as 'an exceptionally important phenomenon in our literature'. He distinguished between light comedy, in which the petty frailties of individuals are held up to ridicule, and high comedy, 'the comedy of civilisation' as he called it, which depicts common social vices. Light comedy serves as an idle distraction, inviting us to laugh at the folly and foibles a man exhibits in his private life, at the plight of some wretched miser, jealous husband, or an old man madly in love. High comedy attacks vices indulged in by man acting in a social capacity, and the laughter it produces is quite different, being commingled with a sense of shame arising from self-recognition. Such laughter, directed not at the offender but at the offence, is socially beneficial; the louder and more maliciously people laugh at public vices, the better for morality. The writer of a social comedy, far from undermining authority, actually increases people's respect for it by exposing abuses. Gogol's play belonged to the second category. In fact it was a new kind of comedy, very different from the classical comedy of manners which reflected the social climate of earlier times.

Androsov went on to draw a distinction in drama between literal truth, or absolute fidelity to real life, and literary truth, which consists in presenting people as human types and showing how, being what they are, they would think and act in particular circumstances, but without any attempt to explain why they so behave, since that is not the dramatist's function. Gogol's comedy was of the latter kind, for it conveyed this inner truth and expressed the essential nature of his fictitious characters, who exemplified the various forms of morals and manners found in provincial Russia. Then, sensing perhaps the political risk involved in accepting Gogol's picture of Russian reality, Androsov asserted, quite against the sense of what he had written before, that it was not in any way typical. He could not understand, he said, why officials and others should take offence at *The Government Inspector*, since its author was attacking individual abuses and presenting characters who were exceptions. Like Gogol himself, Androsov refused to admit the typicality of these characters, hoping thereby to reassure his readers that the play did not in any way pose a threat to the regime.

In *Rumour*, a weekly supplement to the journal *Telescope*, a sympathetic and perceptive review of the Moscow production was published by the editor Nikolai Nadezhdin, under the initials A.B.V.[30] Nadezhdin affirmed that the comedy, despite the malicious attempts of Bulgarin and Senkovsky to discredit it, and notwithstanding the obvious signs of haste in the production, was nevertheless a great success with the general public because

Gogol was a writer of talent and his play was wholly relevant to contemporary life. He had not written a domestic comedy based on the conventional love intrigue, but a social comedy which dealt with real life and real people. It was a thoroughly Russian play, a product not of imitation but of Gogol's bitter feelings about his country. Furthermore, it was a more serious and profound work than many people realised. 'Those who think that this comedy is amusing and nothing more are mistaken,' he wrote. 'Certainly it is amusing, on the surface, so to speak; but inside it is a thing of grief and woe, a poor creature clad in rags and tatters.'[31] The players had mistakenly tried to be funny, whereas they should have acted simply, truthfully and good-naturedly. This quality of good humour, profoundly characteristic of all Gogol's works, was almost entirely missing in the Moscow production. Finally the actors, with the notable exception of Potanchikov (playing the Postmaster), were criticised for gabbling their lines and taking the play altogether too briskly, thus failing to reproduce the leisurely speech and sluggish pace of life one found in the provinces.[32] Even in a grave emergency, such as the one they face in the play, the townspeople would not change the habits of a lifetime: they would still move about quietly and sedately.

Meanwhile, following the uproar his play had caused in St. Petersburg, Gogol decided to leave Russia. In his letter to Pogodin of 10 May he wrote: 'I am going abroad to dispel the anguish that my countrymen are causing me each day. A modern writer, a comic writer, a writer concerned with morals and manners should be as far away from his native land as possible. A prophet is without honour in his own country.' He was in a state of inner turmoil, unable to resolve the deep conflict within him. He felt that he must escape from Russia, for a time at least, in order to see it more clearly from a distance and to reflect on his role as a writer. On 6 June 1836, accompanied by his old schoolfriend Danilevsky, he left for Western Europe.

3. Later Reviews and Revisions

Even before Gogol left Russia attempts were made by influential officials and journalists to have his play banned from the stage or at least performed as infrequently as possible. These attempts came to naught, but soon afterwards the authorities, alarmed by the success of the play, sought to counteract its political impact by arranging for it to be followed by a three-act sequel written, apparently, by a certain Prince Tsitsianov, if not to order at least with official blessing.[33]

In this crudely unrealistic denouement, entitled *The Real Inspector*, justice is seen to be done and the wrongdoers are duly punished, as the dramatic conventions of the time demanded. The real government inspector, a certain Provodov, has been staying in the district town for some time under an assumed name and is acquainted with all that has happened there. In the final scene Provodov announces his engagement to the Governor's daughter and then, after revealing his true identity, proceeds to pronounce sentence on the various officials. The Governor is barred from office for five years and the rest are forced to resign. Most severely dealt with is Zemlyanika, who is to be taken to court for informing on his colleagues. Khlestakov, who returns to town, is condemned to serve as an ensign in a remote province. This sequel, first played on 14 July, was taken off the stage after only a few performances, having been loudly hissed by the audiences.

Gogol saw the Moscow production of *The Government Inspector* on 17 October 1839, during his first visit to Russia after leaving three years earlier. Sergei Aksakov persuaded the director, Mikhail Zagoskin, to put on a special performance in honour of Gogol, who was spending a short time in Moscow. The play was given at the Bolshoi Theatre, to which the Maly production had been transferred in May of the previous year. Many Muscovite notables attended the theatre that evening, among them quite a number of literary figures, and the actors, who included Shchepkin, did their best to excel in the presence of the author. The performance went down well with the audience but not, apparently, with Gogol who sat, or rather slumped, in a box on the pit-tier. At the end of the second act some of the spectators rose and applauded, calling for the author;[34] but Gogol did not show himself. He had earlier asked Sergei Aksakov to inform Zagoskin that he was not in the theatre. This piece of deception annoyed Zagoskin, who knew full well that Gogol was present. Taking him at his word, Zagoskin made no attempt to invite him to the director's box, from which it was customary for authors to take a bow. As the tumultuous cries continued Gogol sank lower in his seat and, after almost crawling out of the box, hurriedly departed. The curtain rose and the actor playing Khlestakov came forward to announce that the author was not in the house. At the theatre exit Gogol was overtaken by Aksakov, who had seen him leave, but he could not prevail upon him to return. The following day he wrote a letter of apology to Zagoskin in which he stated, quite untruthfully, that he had received distressing news from home just before the performance. He was fortunately dissuaded from sending the letter, but his sudden departure from the theatre caused something of a scandal and made a bad impression on the public, who saw it as a sign of vanity on his part. There can be little doubt that Gogol felt piqued at the way Zagoskin had snubbed him, but he probably used this as a convenient excuse for making his escape. Despite his thirst for fame he had a genuine horror of public acclaim. This is borne out by the fact that he reacted in exactly the same way twelve years later when he slipped out of the Maly Theatre half-way through a performance of his play to evade the plaudits.

The Government Inspector steadily gained in popularity, especially in Moscow, where the production was greatly superior to that being shown in St. Petersburg, except when Shchepkin appeared there in April 1838 as a guest artist. By 1839 it was an established theatrical attraction, despite the continued hostility displayed towards it by many people in official circles. Both its popularity and its more frequent appearance on the stage were due in no small measure to the praise bestowed on it by Belinsky, the most famous literary critic of that time.

In a short anonymous article written in 1836 Belinsky referred to the play as 'a genuine work of art' which exhibited qualities already apparent in Gogol's earlier writings, his 'original view of things, his ability to capture character traits and stamp them with the mark of typicality, his inexhaustible humour'. Two years later Belinsky again praised the comedy as 'a profound work of genius' and 'a great work of dramatic genius'. His main critique, however, was embodied in a long article on Griboyedov's *Woe from Wit* which he wrote in the autumn of 1839 and published early the following year in *Notes of the Fatherland*.[35] This detailed study of Gogol's play, the first to appear in Russian critical literature, was written before Belinsky had embraced the philosophy of materialism, at a time when he was still largely committed to Hegel's concept of reconciliation with reality and believed in the autonomy of art. He staunchly maintained that the creative artist should be objective and not allow his moral or political opinions to intrude in his work.

Comedy and tragedy, Belinsky declared, are both based on some dramatic conflict, but whereas tragedy deals with lofty passions and great crimes, comedy is concerned with more trivial passions and misdeeds. A tragic conflict evokes horror, compassion, or a feeling of pride in the dignity of human nature. In comedy, on the other hand, the conflict provokes laughter, a reaction which is not just an expression of mirth on the part of the spectators, but a way of taking revenge at witnessing the degradation of human dignity. Thus the moral law triumphs in comedy, just as it does in tragedy, albeit in a different way. Drama, like all works of art, must be based on an idea. Gogol's play, in Belinsky's view, expressed the idea of 'the negation of life', since it was concerned with 'illusions', by which he meant all that is bad, ugly or unworthy of man's highest spiritual aspirations.[36] What we are shown in *The Government Inspector* is 'a void filled with the activity of petty passions and petty egoism'. Gogol's comedy is a statement of the ideal through its negation – a wholly Hegelian concept. All the feverish activity in the play is illusory; it is a purely negative force, the chaotic element in life struggling against a higher, 'rational' reality.

All the actions in the play, Belinsky observed, are strictly motivated by the characters of the people involved. These people are taken at a critical point in their lives and reveal the essence of their being, so that we can deduce from this one chapter the whole of their previous life-history. Gogol's characters are not puppets, but real people drawn from Russian life. Khlestakov is a shallow, foolish person, foppish in both dress and manners, exactly the kind of dandified figure that adorned signs hanging outside inns, barbers' and tailors' shops in Moscow (aptly described by Belinsky as a денди трактирный). This young man, who reacts unthinkingly to each new situation, is quite innocent of any design to defraud the town officials and at the Governor's house, after a copious lunch and flushed with wine, he prattles away hardly aware that all he says is pure invention. In this role of presumed inspector he is 'a creature of the Governor's frightened imagination, a phantom, a shadow of his conscience'.[37] It is the Governor's fear that sets the play in motion, therefore the Governor is its central character. He is 'no caricature...but an extremely clever person in his own way and very effective in his own sphere of life'. However, his normally shrewd mind is so clouded by fear of exposure and retribution that he 'inhabits a world of phantoms'. His fear is increased by the fact that the inspector has been sent from St. Petersburg, a remote and mysterious world beyond his ken. We are not told anything about his earlier life, but it is clear that he was poorly educated and in his childhood had received no moral or religious guidance. As a youth he was given 'lessons in worldly wisdom, that is to say in the art of *feathering his nest* and *covering his tracks*'. His philosophy is simple and pragmatic. He believes the aim of human life is happiness, which can only be assured by the possession of wealth and rank. To attain these one may use any means to hand, including bribery, peculation and servility towards those with money and power. He is the product of a society that condones such practices and he considers his behaviour to be justified by the fact that everyone else resorts to them.

In Belinsky's judgement, there were no scenes in the play which could be singled out as better than the rest, because there were no inferior ones. It was a true work of art with a unity imposed not by the external form, but by the content. It constituted a self-contained world in which each element formed an indispensable part of an integrated whole. The play thus fulfilled Belinsky's chief requirement of a work of art, namely that it should contain nothing arbitrary or accidental, that everything in it should proceed inevitably from some basic idea and unfold logically from its inner rationale. By contrast, Griboyedov's play *Woe from Wit* had no unifying idea and its dramatic conflict was not inevitable but fortuitous. Although it was highly poetic and contained many fine scenes, *Woe from Wit* did not present a self-contained world but had an extrinsic purpose, namely to ridicule contemporary society. Being a satire, it could not be regarded as a work of art since, according to Hegel's aesthetic, all satire is artistically flawed by its tendentiousness. Similarly Molière's plays, despite their undoubted merits, were not true comedies but satires, for they too were not artistic ends in themselves but 'a means of correcting society by mocking at vices'. Belinsky failed to note that Gogol's play was also a satire, since it was written with the intention of eradicating social abuses by holding them up to ridicule. It is true that Gogol, unlike Griboyedov and Molière, eschewed overt didacticism in his comedy, but his purpose was the same as theirs – to effect a moral reform by means of ridicule. Apparently it did not occur to Belinsky that a satire might be conveyed objectively, as is the case with *The Government Inspector*. Nor does he seem to have considered whether dramas that lacked objectivity, like those of Molière, might nevertheless be works of art. Having ruled out satire, Belinsky took the view that Gogol's play was essentially a psychological study.

Nikolai Grech, a close literary associate of Bulgarin, strongly disagreed with the opinions Belinsky expounded in his article. During the winter of 1839–40 Grech delivered a series of public lectures which were published shortly afterwards under the title *Readings on the Russian Language*. In his tenth lecture he took Belinsky to task for pronouncing *The Government Inspector* greatly superior to *Woe from Wit* and to all of Molière's comedies, a judgement which he described as 'a bitter mockery of both the public and Gogol'. In Grech's estimation *The Government Inspector* was not a comedy but 'a caricature in dialogue' (карикатура в разговорах), in which no ideas and no noble or lofty emotions were expressed. But he was more indulgent towards its author than Bulgarin and Senkovsky had been because he found the play, for all its shortcomings, to be not only amusing, as they had readily allowed, but also witty and gay, with characters that were vividly portrayed and true to life.[38]

Gogol was greatly flattered by Belinsky's article and in his later writings on *The Government Inspector* he developed some of the views first expressed about it by the critic, notably the idea that the Governor's error in mistaking Khlestakov for an inspector springs from an uneasy conscience.[39] But Gogol disagreed fundamentally with Belinsky's opinion that the Governor is the main character in the play. Two years later, in a letter of 20 April 1842, Belinsky withdrew this and conceded that Gogol was right in maintaining that Khlestakov was the central character.[40] Gogol would not have agreed either that there were no inferior scenes in the play. On the contrary, he was far from satisfied with a great deal in the first version of 1836 and completely revised the play in the course of the next six years. He was particularly dissatisfied with the fourth act and he tells us in his *Extract from a Letter* that he sat down immediately after the premiere and began to rewrite the beginning of it, after observing during the performance that the play appeared lifeless at this point and the pace of the action dragged rather limply.[41]

For the next two and a half years he left the text of the play untouched, being preoccupied with his main work, *Dead Souls*. Then towards the end of 1838 he began to alter and correct some of the scenes in Act IV, but completed this revision only in January and February of 1841, whilst he was living in Rome. He asked Sergei Aksakov to supervise the publication of a new edition of the play, incorporating these changes. Aksakov, having just suffered the loss of his youngest son, felt unable to participate in the enterprise and handed it over entirely to Pogodin. The latter, eager to include contributions by Gogol in his new journal *The Muscovite*, took the liberty of publishing the amendments to Act IV in the March issue of 1841, thereby incurring the author's displeasure. Pogodin then pressed ahead and brought out the second edition of the play in the summer of the same year, disregarding Gogol's express wish that it should be delayed until the autumn, when he believed it would attract better sales. In the new version of the play the opening scenes of Act IV were modified and new material was added to them. The most significant change was the addition of a new scene at the beginning of the act, in which the officials are shown conspiring to bribe Khlestakov.

During June and the first half of July 1842, whilst he was staying in Berlin and Bad Gastein, Gogol thoroughly revised his play, using a copy of the first edition specially printed with wide margins. He meticulously worked over the lines, pruning away all superfluous matter to achieve a dense, compact texture and produce 'a pearl of creation', to borrow an expression he used in *Dead Souls*. Having read and heard many comments on his play, he decided to underline its serious social implications. Accordingly he eliminated most of the farcical incidents, which had been grossly overplayed in the original production, and increased the satirical content, thereby giving the play a broader social significance. The comedy in its final form gained considerably in dramatic dynamism and was greatly superior as a work of art to the earlier versions.

The textual changes that Gogol made chiefly affected the speeches of Khlestakov and the Governor, adding greater subtlety and depth to their characterisation. The Governor's speeches in Act I were made shorter and crisper by eliminating extraneous details. So, too, were Khlestakov's speeches in the sixth scene of Act III. On the other hand, Khlestakov's lies and exaggerations were made even more extravagant and the Governor's last main speech in Act V was expanded into a magnificent tirade, culminating in the famous words addressed to the audience: 'What are you laughing at? – You are laughing at yourselves!' The short interview with the N.C.O.'s wife in Act IV, which had been deleted by the censor from the text published in 1836, was restored. Gogol also included detailed directions for presenting the final dumb scene, which had been bungled on the stage, and appended an epigraph as a riposte to his critics. This version of the play appeared in the fourth volume of his collected works, published by Nikolai Prokopovich and dated 1842.[42] Finally, while preparing a second edition of his works in 1851, Gogol made a few minor stylistic changes which are incorporated in the standard text of the play.

In addition to the three published versions of *The Government Inspector* there are numerous manuscripts of all or part of the text, written at various stages of its composition. Among the extant manuscripts are two versions of the play which antedate the first published text of 1836. The work thus exists in five different versions, which will be referred to hereafter as R1, R2 etc., the letter R being used to denote 'Revizor' (the Russian title). These versions, in chronological order, are as follows:

R1 First manuscript draft.
R2 Stage text.[43]
R3 First published text of 1836.
R4 Second published text of 1841.
R5 Third published text of 1842.

4. Gogol's Commentaries

Besides altering and revising the text of *The Government Inspector* several times, Gogol took considerable pains to answer his critics and to elucidate the play for the benefit of the public and the acting profession. His first comments appeared in a spirited defence of it made in a short dramatic sketch entitled *Leaving the Theatre after the Performance of a New Comedy.* He wrote the original draft of this piece, it is believed, in May 1836, and completely revised it in the summer of 1842 for publication in the first edition of his collected works, printed at the end of the same year.

The scene of the sketch is a theatre foyer. The author stands discreetly on one side listening to remarks made about his comedy by the spectators as they leave the theatre. Various people from different walks of life express their opinion in turn. Some of them give the views of the ordinary members of the audience, some voice objections made by Gogol's literary opponents Bulgarin and Senkovsky, others serve as mouthpieces of the author. *The Government Inspector* is generally agreed to be amusing, but is variously condemned as a silly, improbable farce or as a sordid spectacle presenting caricatures of humanity. Society's sores, it is argued, should be concealed from the public gaze and are not a fit subject for a comedy. By exposing corrupt officials to general ridicule the author is undermining the confidence of ordinary people in their government.

There are two main criticisms that Gogol is concerned to answer here, the first being that his play has no real plot. His reply to this objection is given by the Second Art-lover, who says that audiences have grown accustomed to a conventional type of comedy based on a love intrigue which inevitably ends in marriage. His play has no plot in that sense, because he believes the scope of comedy should be broadened to include new themes, such as the pursuit of wealth, position or an advantageous match. The action of a play, he says (echoing Belinsky), should be governed by some idea, some conflict which gives the work a unity and involves not only the main protagonists, as in classical comedy, but all the characters. Comedy can thus be just as suitable a vehicle as tragedy for expressing lofty ideas. He then draws a parallel between the role played by Fate in ancient Greek tragedy and that of the government in modern comedy. Firmly believing that governments exercise authority with divine sanction, Gogol elaborates Vyazemsky's remark that the Russian government was an honest character in the play, although by this Vyazemsky had meant no more than that the Tsar was to be praised for allowing the comedy to appear on the stage. 'A kind of secret faith in the government is harboured in our hearts,' says the Second Art-lover. 'Well, there is nothing wrong in that: God grant that the government may, at all times and in all places, be mindful of its mission to be the representative of Providence on earth and that we may believe in it as the ancients believed in a Fate which overtook transgressors.'

This idea is further developed by a Very Modestly Dressed Man, another mouthpiece of the author, who argues that the play, by exposing corrupt officials, will strengthen the trust of the people in their government. 'Let them dissociate the government from its bad executives,' he says. 'Let them see that abuses come not from the government, but from those who do not understand its requirements and who do not want to be answerable to it. Let them see that the government is noble, that its unslumbering eye watches over all alike, that sooner or later it will catch up with those who have violated the law, honour and man's sacred duty, and that those with guilty consciences will blanch before it.' Clearly Gogol intended the ending of *The Government Inspector* to be seen as a victory for the authorities.

The second main charge which Gogol answers is that there is not a single decent or virtuous character in his play. The reason for this, he explains, is that an honest figure would attract all the sympathy of the spectators and make them forget the wickedness of the other characters, thus spoiling the whole effect. The image of the honest man is presented indirectly or implicitly, by showing his opposite. The Second Art-lover asks: 'Does not all the deviousness of heart, even the slightest, in an ignoble and dishonest person of itself show us what an honest man should be like? Does not all this accumulation of base actions and breaches of law and justice show clearly what is required of us by law, duty and justice?'[44]

At the end the author steps forward and speaks in his own person. Taking up an observation made by Androsov, he expresses regret that the spectators have failed to notice the one truly honest character in the play, namely *laughter*, not the kind that serves merely as an idle distraction, but 'the laughter that springs wholly from man's better nature,...which goes to the heart of things and highlights something that would have gone unnoticed otherwise, and without whose penetrating force man would not be so appalled by the triviality and emptiness of life'. Such laughter does not make us feel angry or vindictive towards the wrongdoer whose baseness is held up to ridicule, but tends to reconcile us with him by moving us to compassion. The wrongdoer himself will not join in the laughter but he will be affected by it, for mockery is something men fear above all else. The concept of laughter as a moral force was for many years a cornerstone in Gogol's aesthetic credo. At this time he still believed that abuses could be corrected by exposing them to ridicule on the stage. Only four years later, however, he expressed a different view in his *Selected Passages*. In one of his letters he declared pessimistically that 'you can achieve nothing by satire', and in another that in Russia 'bribery has reached such proportions that there are no human means of stamping it out'.[45]

Some time after completing his dramatic apologia *Leaving the Theatre* Gogol wrote *A Warning to those who would play 'The Government Inspector' properly*, an essay which was not published until 1886.[46] His chief advice to actors is that they should not caricature their parts but play them naturally, indeed even underplay them, in order to achieve the right comic effect. 'The main thing to guard against is caricature,' he wrote. 'There should be nothing exaggerated or trite, even in the minor roles. On the contrary, the actor should try particularly to be more modest, more simple and noble, so to speak, than the person he is playing really is. The less the actor tries to play for laughs, the more he will reveal the comic nature of the part he is playing. The humour will emerge spontaneously from the very seriousness with which each of the persons portrayed in the comedy is occupied with his own concerns. They are all busily, even feverishly pursuing their own affairs as if these were the most important things in their lives. Only the spectator, from his detached position, can see how futile their concerns are.' Gogol was doing something more here than advising actors how to tackle their parts; he was enunciating one of his fundamental dramatic principles – that the characters should be exposed not by others but by themselves.

The actor's primary task, Gogol continues, is to get under the skin of the character he is playing and find out what makes him tick. 'An intelligent actor,' he writes, 'before seizing on the minor oddities and the minor outward peculiarities of the person he is playing should strive to grasp the *universal human* expression of the character.[47] He should consider why this part was created, examine the principal and overriding concern of each person, the thing he spends his life on and which is the permanent object of his thoughts, his constant preoccupation...He should not worry too much about particular scenes and small details. These will succeed by themselves and be skilfully done provided he concentrates all the time on this preoccupation that possesses the mind of his character.'

The Governor is primarily interested in personal gain, in 'not missing anything that floats into his hands', as his friend Chmykhov puts it in the letter read out at the beginning of the play. Because he has always had an eye to the main chance he has never taken a hard look at life or at himself. For the same reason he has turned into an oppressor almost without realising it, since he is not actuated by any malicious desire to tyrannise over others. Nor is he vindictive, for he forgives the merchants who have informed against him to Khlestakov. Aware of his sins, he prays, goes to church and believes himself to be a devout Christian. He even contemplates reforming some day, but the lure of worldly possessions is too great to resist and the urge to acquire them has become an ingrained habit with him. Confronted in the play with a trickier situation than he has handled before, he oscillates between panic and elation, and his nerves are strained. This affects his judgement and makes it possible for him to be deceived, something most unlikely to happen when he was not under such emotional stress. 'Thus, when it is suddenly announced that a real inspector has arrived, the shock of this thunderbolt is greater for him than for everyone else and his position becomes truly tragic.'

The most difficult role in the play is that of the main character, Khlestakov, whose paramount urge is to show off and impress everyone as the important person he would like to be. The fear of the officials that they may be exposed gives this nonentity a golden opportunity to appear important, but he has no thought of swindling or deceiving them. Even the subjects on which he dilates so extravagantly are all suggested in the first place by his listeners. He is impulsive in everything, and when he talks he is simply carried away by his own imagination, so much so that he believes his own fantasies. 'In short,' writes Gogol, 'he is a phantasmagorical person, the embodiment of lies and deception, who sweeps off in his troika God knows where.' This last remark may well have been suggested by Belinsky's description of Khlestakov as a phantom.

These observations tally with the comments Gogol made earlier in his *Extract from a Letter*, 'Khlestakov is not an impostor at all; he is not a professional liar; he forgets that he is lying and almost believes his own words. He is uninhibited and in high spirits. He sees that everything is going well, that he is being listened to – and for that reasons alone he speaks with greater fluency and familiarity, he speaks with an open heart, absolutely frankly, and in his lying he reveals himself for what he is....Khlestakov does not tell lies at all coldly or in a theatrically boastful way; he lies with passion and his eyes express the pleasure he derives from it. All in all, this is the finest and most poetic moment of his life – almost a kind of inspiration.'

Khlestakov's character, Gogol continues, is fluid and elusive. In appearance he is perfectly ordinary and does not differ in any way from other young men. 'He even behaves well occasionally and speaks at times with gravity. It is only in situations demanding either presence of mind or strength of character that the mean and insignificant side of his nature is revealed...If you analyse Khlestakov, what is he in fact? A young man, a civil servant, and a shallow fellow, as they say, but one who has many qualities possessed by people whom the world does not deem to be shallow...In short, this man should be a type embodying many things found separately in different Russian characters, but here combined fortuitously in one person, as very often happens in real life. Each of us becomes or has become a Khlestakov at least for a moment, if not several moments, only naturally we do not care to admit it. We even like to make fun of the fact, but of course only when we see Khlestakov in someone else, not in ourselves.'[48]

These and other comments on the *dramatis personae* which Gogol published in the two articles quoted above, together with the brief character sketches with which he prefaced the play, and various observations he made in letters to Shchepkin and Sosnitsky, are an invaluable source of guidance for actor and reader alike.

In the autumn of 1846 Gogol wrote *The Denouement of 'The Government Inspector'*, in which he put forward an entirely new interpretation of his comedy. This dramatic tailpiece was written whilst he was finishing his *Selected Passages*, at a time when he was preoccupied with religion and believed he had a messianic destiny to fulfil. He now began to reinterpret his earlier writings retrospectively. In *The Denouement* he asserts that his comedy is not a social satire, but a moral allegory. The provincial town in the play, he explains, is in reality the spiritual city which exists within each one of us. The dishonest officials represent various human passions which dwell there and 'plunder the treasury of our soul', while Khlestakov is the incarnation of our volatile worldly conscience. The play as a whole is intended to arouse in us fear of the real inspector, who symbolises our true conscience and is the voice not of the government, but of the Eternal Judge whom we all have to face in the hour of death.[49] This view of *The Government Inspector* as a kind of secular morality play was clearly an *a posteriori* revaluation of the work on Gogol's part, for he certainly had no such conception of the comedy in mind when he wrote it ten years earlier.

The cast of this dramatic epilogue comprises the players themselves and a few spectators. It opens with 'the leading comic actor' (i.e. Shchepkin or Sosnitsky) being offered a laurel wreath by his fellow-actors and urged to crown himself.[50] The rest of the scene consists of a discussion about the nature of comedy between the leading comic actor and the spectators. One of the latter protests that *The Government Inspector* is of no real benefit to society. Another condemns it as positively harmful and takes particular exception to the Governor's words: 'What are you laughing at? – You are laughing at yourselves!' as an impertinence and a sign of disrespect to the audience. Finally, when one of the spectators asks to know the meaning of the play, the leading comic actor provides the key, explaining that it is not to be taken literally, but as an allegory.

Many of Gogol's friends and admirers strongly objected to this interpretation of *The Government Inspector*. Sergei Aksakov sought to prevent the scene from being published because, as he wrote to his son Ivan, 'It is all ridiculous and absurd nonsense from beginning to end, and if it is published it will make Gogol the laughing-stock of all Russia.' Shchepkin, who had a great affection for both the play and its author, indignantly rejected this new interpretation. After failing, through illness, to answer three of Gogol's letters from abroad he eventually sent a reply on 22 May 1847, in which he protested vehemently that Gogol had reduced the flesh-and-blood characters of his comedy to lifeless abstractions. 'After reading your ending of *The Government Inspector*,' he wrote, 'I was furious with myself at my own short-sightedness, because up till now I have studied all the characters in *The Government Inspector* as living people...Leave them me as they are. I love them, love them with all their weaknesses...You want to take them away from me. But I won't let you have them, not as long as I live! After I've gone you can turn them into goats if you like, but till then I won't part with Derzhimorda, because even he is dear to me.'

Gogol, in reply to Shchepkin's letter, which caused him considerable embarrassment, claimed that the symbolic interpretation referred only to *The Denouement* itself. He admitted, however, that this was a clumsily written piece which would give spectators the mistaken impression that he wished to turn *The Government Inspector* into an allegory. 'That is not what I have in mind,' he wrote. '*The Government Inspector* is *The Government Inspector*, but the essential thing is for each spectator to relate the play to himself, and this applies to every other play besides *The Government Inspector*, though it is more appropriate in the case of *The Government Inspector*.' The whole point of the epigraph was to make the spectator examine himself and see whether his own mug was crooked.

Two months later, in a further attempt to answer Shchepkin's criticism, Gogol rewrote the last part of *The Denouement*. In this so-called *Supplement to The Denouement* the leading comic actor is now made to explain that he is not seeking to impose his own allegorical interpretation of the play on his audience. Nor could the author, had he any such idea in mind when writing the play, have made this obvious, for the result would have been an insipid homily. In fact the author's purpose had been to describe the horror induced by abuses in the real world, not in some ideal or abstract town of the soul, and to show that evil should not be regarded as an essential complement to good, as shade is to light in a picture. His aim was 'to gather together in one pile all the worst things on our earth' and 'to depict the dark side so vividly that everyone should feel it necessary to do battle against it and the spectator be made to tremble, filled with horror at the sight of lawless acts'.

Gogol insists that we should examine our own hearts and apply the moral of the play to ourselves. He bears witness to the wholesome, cathartic power of laughter that is born of love for one's fellow-men. This kind of laughter is a scourge that shames us and drives out the base impulses which steal into our hearts under a noble guise. 'It has been given to us,' he concludes, 'so that we might laugh at ourselves, not at others. And anyone who lacks the courage to laugh at his own failings would do well never to laugh at all. Otherwise laughter will be turned into slander, a crime for which he will be answerable...' This last remark clearly reflects Gogol's sense of guilt, born of the belief that he had sinned by using laughter as a weapon to attack others. He sought to assuage his guilt feelings by suggesting that he had acted charitably towards his fellow-men in showing them their faults and thus enabling them to become better human beings. However, fearing perhaps that this rationalisation would not carry much conviction, he eventually decided not to send the *Supplement* to Shchepkin.

It had been Gogol's intention that *The Denouement* should be given, together with the final version of the play, at benefit performances in Moscow and St. Petersburg for Shchepkin and Sosnitsky respectively. But this was not to be, since Shchepkin flatly refused to act in *The Denouement* and it never reached the censor of the Third Section, having been rejected by the Director of the Imperial Theatres, A.M. Gedeonov, who declared it quite unacceptable for the leading player to be offered a crown by his fellows, since the rules forbade any such demonstration of approval on the stage. Gogol had also planned to bring out a new edition of *The Government Inspector*, including *The Denouement*. He wrote a preface for the edition, in which he announced that the proceeds from its sale would be donated to the poor and gave a list of influential acquaintances in Moscow and St. Petersburg whom he nominated to collect the money and distribute it in accordance with his wishes. In the event, however, he was so disheartened by the opposition of his friends to this plan that he abandoned the idea of publishing the new edition, even though it was passed by the literary censor Nikitenko. In fact *The Denouement* did not appear in print until 1856, when it was included in the second edition of his collected works.

5. Later Productions and Adaptations

The Government Inspector maintained its place on the Russian stage but continued to divide the public for many years. It was especially popular with the younger playgoers. Vladimir Stasov, an eminent art and music critic, recalled in later life the enthusiasm it had aroused among his fellow-students at the School of Law in St. Petersburg when he was a youth. They even put on an amateur performance of the play in October 1839, without costumes or scenery. And some of them, he tells us, went to see it on the professional stage. 'We were all in raptures over it,' he reports, 'as indeed all the young people were at that time. We would then recite whole scenes and long dialogues from it by heart, correcting and prompting each other. In our own and other people's homes we quite often got involved in heated debate with various elderly people (and sometimes, to their shame, not so elderly people) who waxed indignant about the new idol of youth and tried to make out that Gogol's works bore no resemblance to real life, that it was all invention and caricature on his part, and that such people just did not exist, or if they did there were far fewer of them in a whole town than in this comedy of his. Our exchanges were heated and prolonged...but the old people could not budge us one inch, and our fanatical worship of Gogol only grew stronger and stronger.'[51]

Amongst officials *The Government Inspector* sometimes produced the most hostile and violent reactions. On one occasion it gave rise to a scene of such comic absurdity that it might have come straight from the pen of Gogol himself. In 1848 it was playing in Rostov-on-Don to a packed house. Among those present was the local governor, who happened to have a double-barrelled surname like his counterpart in the play. The worthy gentleman was soon bristling with anger at the guffaws of the other spectators, who were looking significantly in his direction. At the end of the first act, unable to contain himself, he leapt on the stage and began to hurl abuse at the actors for daring to lampoon the authorities in public. It was politely explained to him that the comedy was the work of Nikolai Gogol, a famous writer, and that it was played in St. Petersburg. He was even shown a copy of the text but refused to believe these assurances and threatened to have the actors put in prison unless they stopped the play at once and put on something else instead. By now the theatre was in uproar. At this point the manager appeared, set about the governor with a stick and drove him out of the theatre, calling him a churl and an ignorant brute, much to the amusement of the audience. After the governor and his police officers had gone, the performance continued and was a great success. The governor later lodged an official complaint against the actors, but the affair had become so notorious that his superiors rewarded him with a reprimand and subsequently removed him from his post.

A further incident reveals the accuracy with which Gogol had portrayed provincial officials. In a letter he received from Sergei Aksakov in 1849 his friend referred to a performance of *The Government Inspector* in the town of Rybinsk, which his son Ivan had recently attended. The actors had been struck by the similarity beween the stage characters and the local dignitaries who were occupying the front stalls, whereupon a reversal of roles suddenly took place. 'In the middle of the play,' wrote Aksakov, 'the actors, seeing that the spectators resembled the people in the play more than they did themselves, all split their sides with laughter.'

In the provinces prominent officials continued to look upon the play as a seditious work. In 1856 Count A.G. Stroganov, the Governor-General of Novorossiisk and Bessarabia, expressed his view of it in a private letter to the Minister of Education, A.S. Norov: 'I do not know what your Excellency's opinion is of the comedy *The Government Inspector*, but I believe, with the deepest conviction, that in origin, content and spirit it is a copy, *au petit pied*, of Beaumarchais' *Marriage of Figaro*.[52] I do not know whether it has had any beneficial influence or reformed one single briber or cheat. But I am sure that if *The Government Inspector* and its hundreds of followers[53] have not yet, thank God, had such melancholy consequences for Russia as Beaumarchais' work had for France, nevertheless the translations of them have already given rise to many unfavourable criticisms and false judgements of Russia abroad.'[54] Stroganov was alarmed at the pernicious effect he considered Gogol and other writers were having on French attitudes to Russia. In 1854, soon after the outbreak of the Crimean War, *The Government Inspector* had its first foreign performance in Paris, under the title *Les Russes peints par eux-mêmes*. The translator, Eugène Moreau, had taken many liberties with the text and the play was such a flop that it emptied the theatre of every single spectator. This caused something of a scandal in Parisian society at the time, but it was soon forgotten.[57] Stroganov thus greatly exaggerated the effect the play had on public opinion in France. French hostility towards Russia, especially marked since the early 1830s, was fanned rather by such books as the Marquis de Custine's *La Russie en 1839*, Ivan Golovin's *La Russie sous Nicolas 1er*, and Frédéric Lacroix's *Les Mystères de la Russie*, works published in Paris in the 1840s which all presented an extremely unflattering picture of contemporary Russia.

Perhaps the most noteworthy amateur performance of the play was that given on 14 April 1860 by a group of writers, led by P.I. Weinberg, to raise money for the Russian Literary Fund, a society recently founded to assist needy authors and scholars. The role of Khlestakov was taken by Weinberg

himself, and the Governor was played by Pisemsky. Dostoyevsky played
the Postmaster, F.A. Koni took Abdulin, and amongst the other literary figures
appearing as merchants were Apollon Maikov, Dmitry Grigorovich and
Turgenev – the last wearing a frock-coat and pince-nez. The comedy, acted
on a specially constructed stage at a private house in St. Petersburg, was
given to a packed house and received with general acclaim.

A landmark in the stage history of *The Government Inspector* was its
revival at the Alexandrinsky Theatre in October 1870, when it was given
for the first time according to the final published version of 1842. This
production, mounted with scrupulous concern for historical detail, established the play in its classic form, but at the same time turned it into a kind
of theatrical museum-piece, something which could be admired but scarcely
enjoyed. Moreover, the production lacked harmonious teamwork by the
actors, a thing that Gogol always considered essential to success in the
theatre. In fact the show was entirely stolen by the brilliant comedy actor
Vasily Samoilov, who played the minor role of Rastakovsky.[56]

Gogol's definitive text was used again at the Maly Theatre in 1883 and
thereafter was adopted in playhouses throughout the country. Producers
began to pay more attention to historical accuracy in presenting the comedy,
which was now firmly established as the chief classic of the Russian stage.
Such was the case when the Alexandrinsky and Maly Theatres, the two main
exponents of *The Government Inspector*, mounted jubilee productions in
1886 to celebrate fifty years since its premiere. These were distinguished
only by the large number of well-known actors who took part, even in the
minor roles. The production at the Alexandrinsky in 1897 again underlined
the period flavour of the work. By now nearly all the satirical sting had been
taken out of the play, which was treated merely as a picture of the mores of
a bygone age.

This dry, academic approach to the comedy also characterised the
production given at the Alexandrinsky in 1908 to mark the centenary of
Gogol's birth. A break with this tradition came later in the same year,
however, when the play was put on at the Moscow Art Theatre by Konstan-
tin Stanislavsky, assisted by V. Nemirovich-Danchenko and I.M. Moskvin.
The producers sought to breathe new life into the play by exploring it in
greater psychological depth. But, despite some good acting, the production
was dominated by the meticulous care that was taken to reproduce the *realia*
of Russian provincial life in the early 1830s and the result was rather lifeless.
For all that, it had two features which marked a significant shift in the play's
interpretation and which were taken up by later producers. For the first time
Khlestakov was given pride of place over the Governor, who had been
treated previously as the central figure, quite contrary to Gogol's intention.
And there was an attempt to bring out the symbolic aspect of the work,
especially in the finale, showing that the producers had taken note of the
radical reinterpretation of Gogol's writings propounded by some of the literary

decadents and symbolists. Whereas Belinsky, Chernyshevsky and their followers had treated Gogol as a realist, at the turn of the century Rozanov and Merezhkovsky, followed by the poets Annensky, Bely and Bryusov, put forward a completely different view of him as a master of the grotesque, the hyperbolic and the fantastic, whose works had little to do with reality.

After the Revolution of 1917 the theatres opened their doors to audiences of workers and soldiers. In the first few years of the Soviet period producers made no concessions to the new proletarian spectators, but clung to the well-tried method of presenting Gogol's play and continued to give prominence to external features, especially the décor.

The 1920s saw a great revival of interest in Gogol and with it a whole spate of productions of *The Government Inspector*, among them some of the most striking and memorable ever presented. In 1921 a new production was put on at the Moscow Art Theatre by Stanislavsky, who now staged it as a satire without any emphasis on the historical setting. He compressed the action into a single day and introduced a new spatial conception of the play by presenting it on a narrow strip of platform that gradually expanded as the action unfolded. The outstanding feature, however, was the novel interpretation of Khlestakov by Mikhail Chekhov, a nephew of the famous playwright. Chekhov's Khlestakov was a fantastic character with pronounced pathological tendencies. His face was made up to resemble that of a clown. He made strange, jerky gestures, he slavered, spoke incoherently at times, made long pauses in odd places, then shouted almost hysterically. He gnawed enthusiastically at a table-leg during the wooing scenes, dived under the table when the Judge dropped his banknotes, grabbing them with a smile of joy, hid in panic behind Anna's skirts when the Governor appeared in Act IV, went over to a life-size portrait of Nicholas I in the Governor's parlour and adopted the same regal pose. The effect of this *tour de force* was hypnotic. Khlestakov was transformed into a universal symbol of evil, a grotesque embodiment of the spiritual void that Gogol so deeply abhorred. This interpretation owed much to Merezhkovsky's metaphysical view of Khlestakov as a manifestation of the devil, and Chekhov's brilliant but eccentric performance aroused great controversy. It was out of keeping with the rest of the production, but gave a quite new dimension to the part that could not be ignored by other actors cast in the same role.

In 1922 an updated version of *The Government Inspector* entitled *Comrade Khlestakov* was given at the State Theatre of Comedy and Drama in Moscow. Gogol's original was condensed by D. Smolin into three acts, interspersed with other material, including poems by Mayakovsky, while the characters were given functions appropriate to Soviet society. This rather tasteless attempt to modernise the play was not a success with the public. After that came other experimental productions of *The Government Inspector*: a constructivist version by V.M. Bebutov in 1924 and a pantomimic version by N.V. Petrov two years later. But these theatrical curiosities were completely eclipsed by Vsevolod Meyerhold's stupendous production, first staged in December 1926.

This was a lavish spectacle in fifteen episodes, drawn from the different versions of the play and bodied out with material from Gogol's other works. Great liberties were taken not only with the text but also with the *dramatis personae*, who were much increased in number and sometimes formed into a chorus. Gogol's originals were altered and adapted, some of them becoming an amalgam of various characters he had created of the same type. The Governor was turned into a high-ranking officer who struck quasi-Napoleonic poses, while his wife disported herself as a voluptuous society beauty of dubious morals, a kind of provincial Cleopatra. The elderly, taciturn Osip appeared as a sprightly country lad who sang a duet with a maid at the inn. Khlestakov assumed a variety of guises: he was by turns a timid clerk, dreamy poet, astute swindler, imperious general, and dissolute dandy with a hankering after the fleshpots. In the inn scene he cut a demonic, Hoffmannesque figure, dressed in black, with sinister-looking spectacles in square frames and an old-fashioned tall hat. Most of the time he moved silently but rather unsteadily on his spindly legs, and he was accompanied by a wan-faced officer who acted as a silent commentator.[57]

In the last scene the players joined hands and in a dancing file, led by a fiddler, swept into the auditorium, whooping wildly. Then all fell silent as a huge white curtain rose before the stage, bearing the Gendarme's announcement inscribed in large gold letters. It slowly vanished to reveal fully clothed, life-size effigies of the townspeople, arranged exactly according to Gogol's directions for the dumb scene. The substitution of puppets for real people was meant to show the characters of the play as 'dead souls', and the finale was presented in such a way as to symbolise the downfall of the old regime. The production, elaborately orchestrated and mounted with great panache, incorporated the most striking use of décor and lighting, as well as music, dancing and mime. It was a brilliant realisation of the Wagnerian ideal of total theatre, embracing all the arts.

Meyerhold's version of *The Government Inspector*, by far the most striking ever produced, made theatrical history and inspired a voluminous output of critical literature, probably more than any other production of a play before or since.[58] He himself called it 'a grandiose suite on Gogolian themes' and defined its genre as 'musical realism'. In fact it was a sort of *tragédie bouffe* in which the grotesque traits were grossly overdone and the acting overshadowed by the powerful scenic effects. The production toured the provinces and in 1930 was taken to several German towns, then to Paris. Everywhere it provoked great controversy in the press and among the public, greater indeed than the premiere of 1836, and it attracted a good deal more censure than praise. Its director was condemned by leading organs of the Communist Party and denounced on all sides for committing a sacrilege against one of Russia's literary masterpieces, but the production remained in the repertoire right up to 1938, when Meyerhold's theatre was closed.

Other experimental versions of *The Government Inspector* followed in the wake of Meyerhold's bold and imaginative venture. The most bizarre of these was I. Terentiev's futuristic production of 1927, in which Gogol's characters were dressed in emblematic costumes. The Postmaster wore trousers bearing envelopes and stamps, the Doctor had a skull painted on his sleeve, and the Director of Charities bore on his back an image of two strawberries – a reminder of his surname. A new twist was given to the plot by making Khlestakov reappear at the end as the real inspector. But what predominated was the frankly scatological tone, deliberately calculated to scandalise the spectators. Thus, at the centre of the stage was a water-closet to which the actors retired, in Khlestakov's case with a candle and to the strains of Beethoven's *Moonlight Sonata*. This lavatorial approach betrayed the influence of a Freudian study by I.D. Yermakov, who claimed to have discovered in Gogol anal-erotic tendencies.[59]

In the late 1920s a reaction set in against experimental art and in 1934 socialist realism was adopted as the official literary doctrine. With this return to realism modernised versions of *The Government Inspector* fell into disfavour and the play was presented as a brilliant satire on the corrupt tsarist regime. The Maly Theatre production by L.A. Volkov in 1938, a deliberate counterblast to the avant-garde adaptations of the play, was typical of this realistic approach that became the hallmark of nearly all its subsequent appearances on the Soviet stage. An isolated exception was the unsuccessful version presented in 1939 at the Vakhtangov Theatre, in which Gogol's satire was distorted by being treated playfully in an attempt to give the play modern appeal.

To this day *The Government Inspector* has maintained its place as the greatest Russian theatre classic and has had many sucessful revivals, notably at the Maly in 1949 and again in 1952 to celebrate the centenary of Gogol's death. Perhaps the most imaginative production of recent years was that put on at the Maly in 1966 by Igor Ilyinsky, an accomplished Gogolian actor. Appreciating that the vices satirised in Gogol's play are still prevalent in the world today, Ilyinsky sought to bring out its contemporary relevance. He was the first producer to give outward and visible expression to the proverb 'Don't blame the mirror if your mug is crooked', which Gogol took as the epigraph of *The Government Inspector*. These words were broadcast in the foyer and cloak-room of the theatre and repeated, in the same impassive voice, from loudspeakers in the auditorium before the play started. To reinforce the message, the curtain used at the beginning and end of the show took the form of a huge old-fashioned looking-glass, in which the spectators saw their own reflections. Mirrors of various kinds were also placed on the set to create a somewhat grotesque, confused impression. Thus, the actors were reflected in a distorting mirror as they entered the Governor's reception-room. And at the beginning of Act V the Governor, relishing the prospect of high rank, went up to what appeared to be a mirror and saw in it the figure he dreamt of being, in a fine uniform resplendent with epaulettes and a blue cordon across his chest.

The dumb scene was staged in a novel fashion, allowing it to run the full length of time Gogol had prescribed. The curtain fell on the usual tableau after some 10-12 seconds, then the town police-officers appeared on the proscenium in poses similar to those of the main characters, except that they appeared to be falling. This effect, designed to symbolise the tottering tsarist regime, was achieved by means of special clips which secured the actors' boots to the floor. Shortly afterwards the curtain rose again to reveal the principal players against a backdrop of black velvet, and above them appeared replicas in identical poses, expanding and shrinking in size in what seemed like invisible mirrors. Finally the images dissolved and vanished together with the actors, who descended below stage through traps, still frozen in their various postures.

Many generations of Russian actors have been brought up on the play and its roles are treated as touchstones of acting ability. From Sosnitsky and Shchepkin stemmed quite different interpretations of the Governor, to which various modifications were added by later actors. Among the most memorable later interpreters of this role are Vladimir Davydov, Nikolai Yakovlev and Fedor Grigoriev. The part of Khlestakov, one of the most difficult in the Russian dramatic repertoire, was poorly played in the early years, gained in stature with Sergei Shumsky in 1851, and was success-fully realised first by Mikhail Sadovsky in 1877. Since that time the most accomplished exponents of this elusive, chameleon-like character have been Mikhail Chekhov, Stepan Kuznetsov, Erast Garin and Igor Ilyinsky, the last of whom subsequently played the Governor, also with great success. Yet despite all its long experience of *The Government Inspector* the Russian theatre has evolved no generally accepted style of playing Gogol, as it has in the case of Ostrovsky and Chekhov. The play and its characters are still interpreted very differently even within the prevailing realistic tradition.

In addition to its frequent stage appearances *The Government Inspector* has been turned into a film several times. In 1916, during the era of the silent cinema, a Maly Theatre production of the play was filmed by V. Sashin. In 1952 V. Petrov directed a most successful screen version, in which Igor Gorbachev gave a notable peformance as Khlestakov. In 1978 a film adaptation, entitled *The Incognito from Petersburg*, was produced by L. Gaidai. Foreign versions include a Czechoslovak film made in 1933 and one produced in Bombay in 1950, this being an adaptation of the comedy to modern Indian life.[60] The play has also been turned into an opera by composers of various nationalities: by the Czech K. Weis in 1907; by the Russian composer K.N. Shvedov and the Hungarian E. Zádor, both in 1935; by the Italian A. Zanella in 1940, and the German W. Egk in 1957.

The first translation of *The Government Inspector* was Jan Chełmikowski's Polish version, which appeared in 1846. A French translation by Prosper Mérimée was published in 1853[61] and the following year a German one by August von Viedert. The first English translation, by T. Hart-Davies, came out in 1890, followed two years later by that of A.A. Sykes, which included some useful notes and comments. A shortened three-act version of Sykes's rendering was used by the Stage Society in London for the first English performances of the play, given at the Scala Theatre on 17 and 18 June 1906. The first major presentation of the comedy in England was produced by Theodore Komisarjevsky in April 1920 at the Duke of York's Theatre, London, and a few years later at Barnes, using an unpublished translation by T.H. Hall. In America the comedy was first performed in October 1922 at the Yiddish Art Theatre in New York under the direction of Maurice Schwartz, who played the title-role. After this production there followed an English version, given in April 1923 by the Classic Stage Company, with Schwartz again taking the leading part.

Since that time the play has seen many revivals on the stages of the English-speaking world and has been especially popular with amateur companies. Many other translations of it have been made, several specially commissioned for a new production, but the majority of them remain unpublished. Some of the translators have abridged Gogol's five acts to three, and others have even added new characters and inserted material of their own, to such an extent that many acting versions are sheer travesties of the original and descend into pure knockabout farce.

Numerous other translations and adaptations of *The Government Inspector* have appeared in all the major languages of the world and many of the minor ones too. The play has thus attained, in the twentieth century, the status of a great stage classic that belongs to world literature.

6. The Play's Character and Purpose

The Russian stage in Gogol's time was dominated by the virtual monopoly of the Imperial Theatres in St. Petersburg and Moscow. These theatres, which came under the Ministry of the Court, were bureaucratic institutions, in effect an arm of the state. They received a government subsidy, were administered by functionaries and even hired their actors as civil servants.

The spirit prevailing in the Russian theatre was one of almost unrelieved philistinism. For the most part the public was offered a choice between crude vaudevilles, lurid melodramas and turgid historical pieces. Taste was dictated partly by the authorities who promoted plays that fostered public patriotism and loyalty to the crown, and partly by theatre-goers seeking only entertainment. The Tsar himself, who often patronised the theatre, had a great liking for vaudeville, especially for what Turgenev later called 'pseudo-sublime' dramas, though he detested melodrama. The theatrical offerings were mostly translations and adaptations of light comedies by lesser French playwrights such as Ducange, Scribe, Dumas and Marivaux. Audiences also flocked to see the romantic historical dramas of Nestor Kukolnik and Nikolai Polevoi, and above all the pieces of Prince Shakhovskoi and Mikhail Zagoskin, the leading Russian comedy-writers of the period. Seldom did the theatres present plays by Shakespeare, Molière, Schiller and other great dramatists of Western Europe. With the few native plays of real merit things were even worse. The two outstanding romantic dramas of the time, Pushkin's *Boris Godunov* (1825) and Lermontov's *Masquerade* (1835) had to wait many years for their first public performances, while Griboyedov's *Woe from Wit* (1824), a brilliant satire on Moscow society, was permitted on the stage only in a grossly mutilated form until 1869.

Gogol condemned the vaudeville with its inconsequential trivialities and the melodrama with its cheap sensationalism. He voiced his complaints in two articles he wrote just after *The Government Inspector*, one of which was published in *The Contemporary*. Like Belinsky and others before him, Gogol deplored the fact that the theatre was inundated with foreign works and called for a genuinely national repertoire of plays based on Russian life. 'For God's sake,' he wrote, 'give us Russian characters, give us our own people, our rogues and our eccentrics! Onto the stage with them, for everyone to laugh at!' He repudiated the concept of drama as a kind of aesthetic toy, believing it to be a powerful moral force that should be used to influence men for good. 'The theatre,' he declared, 'is a great school and it has a deep purpose: it teaches a living, useful lesson to a whole crowd, a thousand people at one time and...shows us the absurdity of man's habits and vices or the sublimity of his virtues and lofty emotions.'

He rejected the conventional comedy with its hackneyed plot, its artificial dialogue, its cardboard lovers, and its inevitable happy ending. Even Molière's plays, despite their author's great technical skill, seemed to him tedious, long-winded and too schematic. Modern drama, he believed, should reflect the problems of contemporary society and reveal its inner workings, 'the springs that keep it in motion'. 'Nowadays,' says the Second Art-lover in *Leaving the Theatre*, 'a more potent theme for a drama plot is the striving to obtain a lucrative post, to display one's brilliance and eclipse the other man at all costs, to avenge oneself for being ignored or scoffed at. Are not rank, financial capital or an advantageous marriage more dynamic subjects now than love?'

He developed these ideas both in *Leaving the Theatre* and in his *Textbook of Literature for Russian Youth*, written in 1844-5 but not published until 1896. To the frivolous comedies prevalent in his time he opposed serious social comedy, designed to enlighten people as well as entertain them. The kernel of such a play is an idea or theme which gives it shape and unity. The theme must be relevant to contemporary life and its problems, and is best conveyed without explicit moralising. The dramatist should therefore not employ mouthpieces or in any other way seek to foist his message upon the spectator, but must instead allow his play and its characters to speak for themselves. Nor should he impose artificially contrived situations upon his characters; the comic aspect of their behaviour, like all their actions, must spring from within themselves. The characters do not exist for the sake of the plot, but *vice versa.*

The humour of a satirical play is both instructive and destructive, for it enables us to see the truth by attacking those things that degrade man's finer instincts and disfigure him spiritually. As the Young Lady in *Leaving the Theatre* observes: 'There are some of us who are prepared to laugh wholeheartedly at a person's crooked nose but have not the courage to laugh at a person's crooked soul.' The purpose of social comedy is to show us our crooked souls and induce us to make them straight. To be convincing the playwright must draw on real life for his plot and characters, yet he should not slavishly imitate reality in every detail. The serious comedy-writer gives an objective picture of society, but he is not content to be 'a mere recorder of scenes taking place before his eyes, without using them to demonstrate something the world needs to know'. His dramas do not mirror surface appearances; they reflect the underlying nature of things. He selects some ordinary but revealing situation and presents us with what is essential and typical rather than a literal reproduction of life. In short, Gogol believed in artistic realism and rejected naturalism.

He consistently applied these dramatic principles in the plays that he wrote. *The Government Inspector*, unlike nearly all earlier Russian comedies, is based not on a love-plot but an important social problem, namely the corruption practised by the Tsar's administrators. The scenes in which Khlestakov woos the Governor's wife and daughter are pure parodies of the conventional love-plot, and there is no happy ending. Gogol dispensed with the stock figure of the *raisonneur*, whose function in traditional comedy was to act as the voice of morality: there are, however, some traces of the *raisonneur* in the character of Osip and even the Governor, as Gogol himself explains in his introductory observations.[62] He further shunned the dramatic cliché by rejecting the crude, unrealistic division of characters into good and bad, presenting instead a collection of petty knaves. And finally Khlestakov, unlike his counterpart in previous comedies of mistaken identity, is no true impostor but a rather dull-witted young man who assumes a false role without realising it for a long time.

Nevertheless, Gogol did not depart entirely from the established dramatic canons; he retained, for example, the time-honoured conventions of the soliloquy and the aside. He also observed the classical unities of time, place and action, from which the play derives its compact structure and concentrated vigour. The events in the play, it is true, are spread over two days, but they move rapidly and could easily be encompassed within the space of twenty-four hours, as the rules of drama then required. The location is a district town situated in the very heart of Russia, and the scene shifts only between the Governor's house and the local inn. Lastly, the action itself is all of a piece, involving every character directly or indirectly, without the complication of any sub-plot or side issue. The play could well be described, in fact, as a broadly but not wholly realistic comedy with symbolic overtones, set in a neo-classical framework.

In his *Author's Confession* Gogol singles out *The Government Inspector* as a turning-point in his creative life, stating that it was the first work in which he had tried to exert a moral influence on society and in doing so became convinced that he had found his true vocation as a writer. In his early tales of Ukrainian life, he tells us, his humour had been gay and light-hearted. But then, under the influence of Pushkin, he came to take a more serious view of literature and decided to turn his comic gifts to satirical ends.[63] 'I realised,' he wrote, 'that in my writings I had been laughing gratuitously, to no purpose, without knowing why myself. If one is going to laugh it is far better to have a good laugh, and at something that really deserves general ridicule. In *The Government Inspector* I decided to gather in one heap all the bad things I then knew to exist in Russia, all the injustices committed in places and cases where above all justice is required of man, and to ridicule everything at one go. But as we all know, this had a shattering effect. Behind the laughter, which had never before been so powerful in my writings, the reader could sense the sadness.'[64]

Significantly, there is no suggestion here of the allegorical meaning Gogol had attached to his play only a year earlier in *The Denouement*. Instead he now claimed, with typical exaggeration, that his comedy contained an exposure of all the evils then abounding in Russia.[65] Yet the greatest social evil of the time, the system of serf-owning, is nowhere even mentioned in the play, much less exposed or ridiculed, as it had been previously, for example in two comic operas, Knyazhnin's *A Mishap with a Carriage* (1779) and Krylov's *The Coffee-grinder* (1783). The plain fact is that Gogol did not look upon serfdom as an outrage against human dignity. Moreover, as Chernyshevsky later observed, the satire on officialdom in *The Government Inspector* is comparatively mild.[66] Knowing that the censors would not allow him to tackle the really important bureaucrats of St. Petersburg, Gogol had to content himself with portraying a group of ordinary provincial officials who are dishonest and devious, but far from being black-hearted villains. He was much less bold and outspoken in his condemnation of bribery than I. Sokolov had been in his comedy *The Judge's Name-day* (1781) and V. Kapnist in his satirical verse drama *The Slanderer* (1798).

Bribery is the chief abuse that Gogol was attacking in his play, yet it is handled in a curiously ambiguous fashion, without any of the collusion one normally finds in such dealings. It is a peculiar, one-sided kind of bribery in which Khlestakov asks the town officials for financial assistance and takes their bribes on the understanding that these are loans, though it is very doubtful whether he seriously intends to repay them later. When the merchants press him to take a silver tray together with their 'loans' he accepts, but when they offer him sugar and wine he rejects these as bribes. It is the shrewd, practical Osip who snaps them up, for all is grist that comes to his mill.

Gogol's claim, in 1847, that he wrote *The Government Inspector* with the purpose of exerting a beneficial influence on Russian society by exposing its ills is a far cry from the statement he made eleven years earlier, in his letter to Pushkin, that he intended to write a comedy that would be 'funnier than the devil'. To be sure, the two aims are not necessarily incompatible, since the satirist relies on humour, the humour of ridicule, as the chief weapon in his armoury. It is clear, however, that when he began to write his play Gogol conceived it as a light comedy and had little or no thought of changing the hearts of his countrymen and bringing about a moral reform. Two years earlier, in 1833, he had abandoned his satirical comedy *The Order of Vladimir, Third Class*, rightly suspecting that it would run foul of the censor since it touched the powerful bureaucracy of St. Petersburg. 'There is nothing for it but to invent the most innocent plot that even a police-sergeant couldn't be offended by,' he wrote to Pogodin at the time. 'But what is a comedy,' he added, 'without truth and malice!' Accordingly he proceeded to write something totally innocuous, his improbable farce entitled *The Suitors*, but put it on one side, feeling that it was not yet ready for the stage.

In a similarly light-hearted mood he then embarked on *The Government Inspector*, producing in the first draft an amusing comedy full of farce, strong caricature and exuberant gaiety, something very similar in style to the vaudevilles then enjoying a great vogue in the Russian theatre. He continued working on the play for several months, during which time his conception changed into something altogether more ambitious and profound as he came to appreciate the full potentialities of his theme, one capable of demonstrating his firm conviction that works of art can influence men for good. In like manner *Dead Souls*, which he began in the same year as *The Government Inspector*, gradually evolved in the process of composition from a gay, picaresque novel, conceived without any moral purpose, into a grand epic 'poem' which, when completed, would lay bare the very soul of Russia and compare in scope with Dante's immortal trilogy.

By the time *The Government Inspector* was ready for stage presentation and publication it had been transmuted, in conformity with Gogol's new and deeper purpose, from a hastily written near-vaudeville into a well-made satirical comedy which bore only a few residual traces of farce. But despite Gogol's alterations and excisions the play was generally taken to be a farce and his moralistic intention, as we have seen, went almost wholly unnoticed. After seeing his comedy treated as a mere farce by so many people, and especially by most of the actors, Gogol was so disgusted that he put it aside for a few years. He later rewrote a good half of the play, paring down the farcical episodes even further and increasing its satirical content. Yet for all the artistic refinements he introduced into the work he in no way altered its essential character, which had already crystallised in the stage and published versions of 1836. He was thus substantially correct in stating that he had intended the play to be morally illuminating as well as diverting. This had not been his original aim, it is true, but it was soon to become the purpose inspiring it after the initial draft was completed. In this instance, at least, he was not seeking to impose on his play something which was never in his mind at any stage of its composition, as he had done previously in *The Denouement*.

In *Leaving the Theatre*, and in the letter he wrote to Pogodin on 10 May 1836, Gogol claimed to be portraying officials whose illegal conduct was an exception to the general rule. This was plainly untrue, for he knew as well as everyone else that the vast majority of Russian officials practised bribery and corruption. Indeed, some years later he showed great interest in an honest official whom his mother had met in Kharkov.[67] In claiming to have presented exceptional cases he was evidently motivated by a deep feeling of alarm at the political construction put on his play. Most people regarded it as an attack on the Russian system of government, while for him it was no more than a denunciation of corrupt men.

In a letter to Zhukovsky, written at the end of 1847, he recalled the public reaction when his play first appeared. 'People began to see in the comedy a desire to ridicule the legitimate order of things and governmental forms, whereas it was my intention to deride only arbitrary departures by some persons from the regular and lawful order. The performance of *The Government Inspector* made a painful impression on me. I was angry both with the spectators, who misunderstood me, and with myself, who was to blame for their failure to understand me.' Gogol refers here to the malpractices of 'some persons', apparently still unwilling to acknowledge that corruption was the general rule among bureaucrats and not confined to a few individuals. He came nearer the truth in an essay on Russian poetry and drama which he included in his *Selected Passages*. Here he singled out Fonvizin's *The Minor* and Griboyedov's *Woe from Wit* as genuine social comedies which did not indulge in 'light-hearted mockery of the absurd aspects of society', but exposed its 'wounds and diseases, its grave internal abuses with the ruthless power of irony'. These comedy-writers, he stated further on, 'rose up not against an individual, but against a whole host of abuses, against the deviation of a whole society from the right path'. Although these remarks refer to Gogol's predecessors, they provide the key to his own purpose in *The Government Inspector*. At the time he wrote his play Gogol, like Fonvizin and Griboyedov, subscribed to the dictum *ridendo castigat mores.*

On reading *Selected Passages* the radicals and liberals among Gogol's admirers, such as Belinsky, Herzen and Turgenev, concluded that he had reneged on his former progressive views and become a political turncoat. This was a complete misconception on their part, however, for Gogol's political outlook, like his religious convictions, remained substantially the same throughout his life. The evidence of his close acquaintances and of his own writings, including his correspondence, leaves no doubt that politically he was always a conservative. Even as a schoolboy in 1827 he showed himself to be a legitimist and monarchist, and he expressed the same attitude towards political authority in the historical essays he published in *Arabesques* and in his dramatic fragment *Alfred*. He accepted the social order existing in Russia and believed in the strict observance of the country's laws. In his opinion the imperfections of the state machine were not the result of bad laws or of an unjust order but were due entirely to human failure.[68] This was exactly the view taken by the Russian moralists and satirists of the eighteenth century. In the words of Dobrov in Kapnist's *The Slanderer*: 'The laws are sacred, but those who administer them are evil villains' (Законы святы, но исполнители − лихие супостаты).

Gogol's moral aim in writing *The Government Inspector* was to persuade state officials to behave with scrupulous honesty. The finale of the play was intended to show that dire consequences would befall those who disobeyed the law. It was meant to be seen as a triumph for the government, a victory for justice; but this was not how most of his contemporaries interpreted the ending. The whole logic of the play – and indeed the realities of Russian life –

Notes to Part One

1. All dates are given in the Old Style, i.e. according to the Julian calendar, which in the nineteenth century was twelve days behind the Gregorian calendar used in the West.

2. The word 'вор' then signified not only 'thief', but was applied to any criminal. The first letter was branded on the forehead and the other two on the right and left cheek respectively. In 1846 the brand B-O-P was replaced by K-A-T, an abbreviation of каторжник ('convict').

3. *tchins* (чины), i.e. high rank.

4. Quoted by D. Mackenzie Wallace in his book Russia, London, 1877, p. 445.

5. V.A. Sollogub, 'Из воспоминаний' *Русский архив*, 1865, p. 744.

6. O.M. Bodyansky, 'Дневник', *Русская старина*, Oct. 1889, No. 10, p. 134. It has been discovered from local archives that a retired second lieutenant, Platon Volkov, was the person who masqueraded as an inspector in Ustyuzhna. Gogol probably heard of this incident when he worked as a tutor in the house of General P.I. Balabin, who had received confidential information about Volkov's activities. See V.Panov, 'Еще о прототипе Хлестакова...' *Север*, 1970, No.11, pp.125-7.

7. A.S. Pushkin, *Полное собрание сочинений*, Moscow & Leningrad, 1937-49, Vol. 8, Book 1, p. 431.

8. V.I. Shenrok, *Материалы для биографии Гоголя*, Moscow, 1892-7, Vol. 1, p. 364.

9. A.I. Wolf, *Хроника петербургских театров*, St. Petersburg, 1877, Part I, p. 49.

10. A.O. Smirnova, *Автобиография*, Moscow, 1931, p. 331.

11. See N.V. Drizen, *Драматическая цензура двух эпох, 1825-1881,* Petrograd, 1917, pp. 41-3.

12. The theatre, designed by the architect Carlo Rossi and named after the Emperor's consort Alexandra, was opened in 1832. It is now called the Pushkin State Academic Theatre (Государственный академический театр им. Пушкина).

13. Сенная площадь, at that time the haymarket of St. Petersburg.

14. *Исторический вестник*, Sept. 1883, p. 735. Curiously enough, no topknot appears in Karatygin's portrait of Gogol, sketched at the same time.

15. Many scholars treat this remark as apocryphal.

16. P.V. Annenkov, *Воспоминания и критические очерки*, Vol. I, St. Petersburg, 1877, p. 193.

17. Gogol wrote 'у меня на душе так смутно', using the word 'смутный', as he often did in his earlier writings, in its Ukrainian sense of 'sad'.

18. *An Extract from a letter written by the author to a certain writer shortly after the performance of 'The Government Inspector'* was first published in *Москвитянин* in 1841. Writing to Sergei Aksakov from Rome in the same year, Gogol stated that this was part of a letter he wrote on 25 May 1836 to Pushkin, who had missed the premiere, being out of the capital (he had gone to bury his mother near the family estate of Mikhailovskoye, but was back in St. Petersburg, probably unknown to Gogol, between 24-29 April, when he left for Moscow). The letter was not dispatched at the time, Gogol explained, because the poet had returned to St. Petersburg shortly afterwards (he returned from Moscow on the night of 23 May). Some scholars, following Tikhonravov, claim that the bulk of this extract was written early in 1841, and hence not addressed to Pushkin. On balance it seems more likely that Gogol wrote the letter in 1836 and merely polished it up in 1841 for publication. See A.G. Gukasova, 'Отрывок из письма, писанного автором вскоре после первого представления "Ревизора" к одному литератору', *Известия АН СССР, отделение литературы и языка*, 1957, Vol. 16, No. 4, pp. 335-45.

19. *Русская старина*, 1902, No. 7, pp. 100-1. The term 'young Russia' refers to the young writers of the time, especially those who contributed to Pushkin's journal *The Contemporary*. It was doubtless suggested by the names 'Jeune France' and 'Junges Deutschland', used to describe French and German literary movements in the 1830s.

20. See E.S. Kulyabko, 'Из архива АН СССР. Несостоявшееся премирование Гоголя', *Русская литература*, 1967, No. 4, pp. 170-3.

21. *Литературные прибавления к Русскому инвалиду*, 1836, No. 59-60, pp. 475-80.

22. *Северная пчела*, 1836, No. 97, pp. 385-8 and No. 98, pp. 389-92.

23. V.I. Shenrok, in his *Материалы для биографии Гоголя*, Moscow, 1892-7, Vol. 3, p. 483, incorrectly interprets Bulgarin's remark as applying to the whole play. N.A. Kotlyarevsky, in his *Н.В. Гоголь*, Petersburg, 1908, p. 330, and E.L. Voitolovskaya, in her *Комментарий*, 1971, p. 44, repeat the same error.

24. *Библиотека для чтения*, May 1836, Vol. 16, No. 5, pp. 1-44. The review was long considered to be Senkovsky's own, but his authorship has

been questioned by two scholars. L.Ya. Ginzburg ascribes it to the critic
Nikolai Polevoi (*Очерки по истории русской журналистики и кри-
тики*, Leningrad University, 1950, Vol. 1, p. 334); A.S. Dolinin suggests
it was written by Vasily Ushakov, a close friend of Polevoi (*Ученые записки
Ленинградского пед. института, факультет литературы и языка*,
Vol. 18, 1956, No. 5, p. 55). Both scholars agree, however, that Senkovsky
edited the article to suit his own purposes.

  25. *Современник*, July 1836, Vol. 2, pp. 285-309.

  26. The complete saying runs: 'Fear has big eyes, but they see nothing'
(У страха глаза велики, да ничего не видят).

  27. D. Magarshack, in his *Gogol: A Life*, 1957, p. 148, writes that Gogol
'was fortified by the storm his play had raised' and 'his faith in the moral
influence of art now seemed to have been confirmed'. The opposite is the
case; Gogol's faith in the moral power of art was badly shaken by the way
his play was received.

  28. S. T. Aksakov, *История моего знакомства с Гоголем*, Moscow,
1960, pp. 40-1. Tolstoy, nicknamed 'the American', was a notorious
gambler and swashbuckler, satirised in Griboyedov's *Горе от ума* (Act
IV, Sc. 4) and by Pushkin in his second verse epistle *К Чаадаеву* (1821).

  29. *Московский наблюдатель*, May 1836, Part 7, No. 1, pp. 120-31.

  30. 'Театральная хроника', *Молва*, 1836, No. 9, pp. 250-64. This article
was formerly attributed to Belinsky, although he explicitly disclaimed its
authorship, while expressing his agreement with most of the reviewer's
observations. See S. Osovtsov, 'А.Б.В. и другие', *Русская литература*,
1962, No. 3, pp. 75-101.

  31. Nadezhdin's words, which defy exact translation, are: 'но внутри это
горе-гореваньице, лыком подпоясано, мочалами испутано'.

  32. This criticism, though sound in general, does not apply in the case
of Bobchinsky and Dobchinsky, who are supposed to speak rapidly, as
Gogol makes clear in his notes on characters and costumes.

  33. See A. Petrov, 'Николай I как репертуарный цензор: "Настоящий
Ревизор"', *Советский театр*, 1930, No. 5, p. 44, and S.S. Danilov, *"Ревизор"
на сцене*, Kharkov, 1933, p. 43.

  34. Some eye-witnesses put this at the end of the second act, others at
the end of the third. See *Литературное наследство*, Vol. 58, Moscow,
1952, pp. 568-73; I.I. Panayev, *Литературные воспоминания*, Leningrad,
1950, pp. 175-6; S.T. Aksakov, *История моего знакомства с Гоголем*,
Moscow, 1960, p. 59.

  35. *Отечественные записки*, 1840, Vol. 8, No. 1, pp. 1-56.

  36. Belinsky used the term 'illusions' or 'illusoriness' (призрачность) to denote 'the negative aspects of reality', not 'unreality', as some critics have assumed..

37. V. Erlich, in his *Gogol*, 1969, p. 105, makes nonsense of this observation by taking it to mean that Belinsky was 'questioning Khlestakov's very existence'.

38. N. Grech, *Чтения о русском языке*, St. Petersburg, 1840, Part 2, pp. 138-42.

39. This was first pointed out by Pavel Annenkov in his *Замечательное десятилетие* (1880); see P.V. Annenkov, *Литературные воспоминания*, Moscow, 1960, p. 184. But Annenkov was wrong in stating that Gogol was also indebted to Belinsky for the suggestion that laughter plays a positive role in the comedy. Gogol's conception of 'serious' laughter was developed from an observation made by Vyazemsky on Fonvizin's plays and more especially from Androsov's comments on *The Government Inspector*.

40. In making his original assessment of the relative importance of the two characters Belinsky was no doubt influenced by the poor showing made by the actors playing Khlestakov at that time. Gogol himself complained to Sergei Aksakov that he could find no actor suitable for this part, that consequently the play lost its point and should be entitled *The Governor*, rather than *The Government Inspector*.

41. Some of Gogol's biographers are sceptical about his statement that he set about this revision straight after the performance and believe that he started it later.

42. The edition, printed in 1842, was not published until the end of January 1843. Volumes III and IV were held up by the censorship committee which took alarm when Nikitenko, who had passed the collected works, was put under token arrest for one night after allowing the publication of a tale that contained passages considered disrespectful to the army.

43. This exists only in copies, not in Gogol's own hand. From these copies Nikolai Tikhonravov reconstructed the 'original stage text', published in 1886. Tikhonravov believed that two different versions were written between R1 and R3, but V.L. Komarovich, the textual editor of the Soviet Academy edition of the play, established that the various manuscripts belonging to this stage of its composition constitute essentially one version. The texts of this version (R2), used for the original productions in St. Petersburg and Moscow, differ in some details because Gogol made some amendments after he had sent it to Moscow. These slightly divergent texts, and not the published version (R3), were used in the theatres of the two capitals for many years. The final published version (R5), banned from public performance by the censor of the Third Section, was first used on the St. Petersburg stage in 1870, and in Moscow not until 1883.

44. Belinsky made the same point when he wrote in 1841: 'In a comedy we are shown life as it is in order that we might clearly conceive life as it should be.' He went on to cite *The Government Inspector* as a superb example of an artistic comedy (*Разделение поэзии на роды и виды*).

45. The same despairing view of bribery is expressed in the last fragment of the unfinished second part of *Dead Souls*, by the Governor-General. 'I know,' he says, 'that wrongdoing cannot be eradicated by any means, by any terrors or punishments; it is too deeply entrenched. The dishonest business of taking bribes has become a need and a necessity, even for people who were not born to be dishonest.'

46. This essay was probably written about 1846, not in 1842 as Gogol's earlier biographers believed.

47. In a letter to Shchepkin, written in December 1846, Gogol offered advice to actors in almost exactly the same words, saying that they should perceive 'the universal human expression' (общечеловеческое выражение) of their parts. The close similarity of the wording supports the view that *A Warning* was written about 1846.

48. The radical publicist Alexander Herzen wrote in similar vein of 'the eternal type of Khlestakov, recurring from the rural district clerk right up to the Tsar' (Diary, 20 February 1843). The novelist Ivan Goncharov went further, seeing Khlestakov as a universal type. 'Khlestakovs still exist today,' he wrote, 'and perhaps always will exist, not just in Russian society but in human societies everywhere, only in a new form' (*Воспоминания*, II, 5).

49. Gogol's deep, almost morbid concern with the question of man's ultimate accountability to God first appears in a letter he wrote to his mother on 2 October 1833, where he recalls the profound impression made on him as a boy by her vivid, terrifying account of the Last Judgement.

50. When he introduced this gesture of tribute, Gogol may well have recalled attending a performance at the Théâtre-Français, Paris, in January 1837 to mark the anniversary of Molière's birth. At the end of the play the actors had come on the stage in pairs and placed wreaths on a bust of the famous French dramatist.

51. *Русская старина*, 1881, No. 2, pp. 417-18.

52. *The Marriage of Figaro* (1784), in which Beaumarchais exposed dishonesty and incompetence in high places, was often referred to as 'the prologue to the French Revolution'.

53. The followers referred to were all admirers of Gogol's literary talent and particularly the writers who belonged to what the critic Chernyshevsky called 'The Natural School'.

54. "*Литературный музеум*". *Цензурные материалы*, ed. by A.S. Nikolayev and Yu.G. Oksman, 1921, Vol. I, p. 352.

55. A detailed account is given of its reception in E.S. Nekrasova,

'Гоголь пред судом иностранной литературы 1845-1885', *Русская старина*, Sept. 1887, pp. 562-6.

56. In the two main published versions of the play (R3 and R5) this part consists of only a few lines, but Gogol originally included in Act IV a whole scene between Rastakovsky and Khlestakov. He later deleted it because, as he said himself, it slowed down the action, and probably also because Khlestakov, uncharacteristically, came off second best in the encounter. In 1841 this scene was published in *The Muscovite* and as an appendix to the second edition (R4), being intended for reading only. But when it was first introduced on stage in the 1870 production it found such favour with the actors that they kept it in the play for many years.

57. Meyerhold was criticised for introducing, in this shadowy figure, a 'mystical' element into the play. In fact the officer, who was the infantry captain mentioned in Act II, Sc. 3, was included simply as a means of overcoming the artificiality of the soliloquy by providing a listener. See Erast Garin, *С Мейерхольдом*, Moscow, 1974, pp. 127-8.

58. Besides numerous articles three books are devoted solely to this production, viz., A.A: Gvozdev et al., *"Ревизор" в Театре имени Вс. Мейерхольда*, Leningrad, 1927; E.F. Nikitina (ed.), *Гоголь и Мейерхольд*, Moscow, 1927; D.L. Tal'nikov, *Новая ревизия "Ревизора"*, Moscow-Leningrad, 1927. For the fullest account in English see N.Worrall, 'Meyerhold directs Gogol's "Government Inspector"', *Theatre Quarterly*, Vol. 2, No. 7 (1972), pp. 75-95.

59. I. D. Yermakov, *Очерки по анализу творчества Н.В. Гоголя*, Moscow-Petrograd, 1924.

60. The play was adapted for the cinema in 1934 by Mikhail Bulgakov, in collaboration with a producer named Korostin, but this version was never filmed. The script was published in *Новый журнал*, New York, 1977, No. 127, pp. 5-45.

61. The French novelist did not really understand the play and his translation was later subjected to much criticism and correction. See H.Stolze, 'Mérimées "Inspecteur Général", in his *Die französische Gogolrezeption*, 1974, pp. 21-32.

62. Gogol was not the first Russian dramatist to exclude the raisonneur. This artificial, rather tedious personage had been abandoned at least thirty years earlier by Krylov and others.

63. Gogol states that he turned to satirical humour in 1835, after publishing *Mirgorod*, but there were signs of this change at least two years earlier when he started his comedy *The Order of Vladimir, Third Class*. Moreover, he was influenced in this direction not only by Pushkin, but by Belinsky and other literary critics of the time, such as Polevoi. This is convincingly demonstrated by V.V. Gippius at the beginning of his essay *Проблематика и композиция*

"*Ревизора*"(1936), an English translation of which is given in R.A. Maguire's *Gogol from the Twentieth Century* (1974), pp. 216-65.

64. This last observation was probably inspired by the remark Nadezhdin made in his review about the sadness concealed beneath the surface of the play.

65. Gogol made similar extravagant claims for his *Dead Souls*. In his letter to Pushkin of 7 October 1835 (where he asked for a drama plot) he wrote: 'In this novel I want to show the whole of Russia, at least from one side.' And a year later he wrote to Zhukovsky: 'All of Russia will appear in it.'

66. The comment was made in a review of P.A. Kulish's edition of Gogol's works and letters (1857). See N.G. Chernyshevsky, *Полное собрание сочинений*, Moscow, Vol. 4 (1948), pp. 655-6.

67. In a letter dated August 1842 he asked his mother to tell the official that 'his nobility and honest poverty amidst those who grow rich by unlawful acts will find a response deep down in every noble heart'. In his *Parting Words* (Letter 30 of *Selected Passages*) he offered similar encouragement to an official who refused bribes.

68. This opinion is most clearly articulated in his first written response to Belinsky's famous letter from Salzbrunn. Gogol's long reply, which he tore up, was later reconstituted from the fragments by his first biographer, P.A. Kulish.

Part Two

Structure, Style and Characterisation

The excellence of *The Government Inspector* lies in its artistic unity, its vivid delineation of character, and its rich variety of style. In construction, characterisation and dialogue it is a masterpiece of dramatic skill. With the Governor's terse opening announcement the spectator is plunged *in medias res*, his curiosity at once aroused. These few words set the tone for the whole play, bursting upon the assembled officials with explosive force and striking in their hearts a panic fear which provides the impetus for the ensuing events.

The pace of the action varies throughout the play. After the bombshell at the beginning the first act proceeds fairly slowly for a time, as the true state of affairs in the town is revealed by the instructions the Governor issues in order to pull the wool over the eyes of the visiting official by creating a façade of good order in the spirit of the famous 'Potemkin villages', erected fifty years earlier to deceive Catherine the Great. The action gathers momentum again after Bobchinsky and Dobchinsky report seeing Khlestakov at the inn and the Governor is galvanised into a flurry of activity. Acts II and III move at a leisurely tempo in their central scenes (II.8 and III.6) and more rapidly elsewhere. In Act IV a varied pace helps to avoid the monotony of repetition in the bribery scenes, then comes a swift development in the last part, leading to its culmination in Khlestakov's departure. After this the first seven scenes of Act. V move slowly, to be followed by the Governor's sudden collapse in his very hour of triumph – a typically Gogolian *peripeteia* which strikes a note of genuine tragedy at the end.

Gogol, a master of stagecraft, paid the most scrupulous attention to the structure of his comedy and carefully composed the words and actions of all its characters. The play contains several unexpected turns, each of which propels the action forward until in the last act the plot moves inexorably to its climax and resolution, when the scales fall from the eyes of the townspeople. Thus interest is maintained as one comic situation succeeds another, with mounting tension, in a closely knit sequence. The development of the dramatic conflict, given the characters of the people involved, flows naturally and inevitably from the situation in which they find themselves, and there are no loose ends left untied at the finish. The play, with its remarkable compactness, forms an artistic whole, displaying both dramatic and psychological unity.

The comedy is founded on mutual fear and misunderstanding, and this is reflected in the very structure of the play, its exposition being divided between the protagonists. In the first exposition (Act I, Sc. 1-3) the Governor and his associates reveal a picture of their malfeasance in office. In the second exposition (Act II, Sc. 1-7) Khlestakov is presented, mainly through the wry observations of his manservant, following a procedure long established in comedy. Both expositions end on a note of tension; in the first the Governor learns of Khlestakov's sojourn at the inn and in the second Khlestakov is informed of the Governor's arrival on a 'courtesy call'. In each instance one misapprehends the reason for the other's presence.

There is an elegant symmetry in the design of the play. Its conclusion is as brief and dramatic as its opening; it closes, as it begins, with a group scene in which the arrival of an inspector is announced. The reading of a letter precipitates the denouement, just as the reading of a letter launches the action. Thus at the end of the comedy the dramatic wheel has turned full circle, as the officials are transfixed with horror in the face of a catastrophe that seems about to repeat itself.

The play presents, in Belinsky's words, 'a self-contained world', except for a brief time near the end, when Khlestakov's letter is read out aloud before the assembled company. Each official, on hearing the mocking description of himself, disclaims the likeness. The reading of the letter serves to hold up a mirror to each of the guilty men. Having lost face with their fellows on stage, the Postmaster, Zemlyanika and Khlopov in turn appeal to the spectators for sympathy. The Governor goes further, addressing the whole world, all Christendom, then, stepping outside the confines of the play, he rounds on the members of the audience and flings the laughter back in their faces. Metaphorically speaking, he holds the comedy up as a mirror and the spectators see themselves as the 'mugs' to which Gogol refers in his epigraph. At this, perhaps the most powerful moment of the play, the barrier falls between the stage and the audience, making them one, and though it rises again soon after, a significant symbolic act has been performed, whereby the spectators are compelled to look not outwards, but inside themselves. Laughter permeated with the shock of self-recognition has a cathartic effect.

The denouement of the play poses a difficult problem from the artistic point of view. The Gendarme's arrival, giving a final twist to the plot, is a brilliant *coup de théâtre*, but it fails to fulfil Gogol's avowed aim of showing the law triumphant in catching up with the offenders. The author's purpose could have been made unmistakably clear only if he had ended the play with the actual appearance of the real inspector and the dispensation of justice or with a speech in praise of the government or honesty – blatantly moralistic intrusions of kind Russian audiences had come to expect, but which he wished to avoid at all costs. As it is, what Gogol describes as 'the electric shock' produced by the final words leaves the situation unresolved, for justice may in fact be done, but it is not seen to be done. The idea of retribution or nemesis does not take tangible shape, for the Gendarme's words may be taken to mean that the law will be upheld or equally be seen as heralding a recurrence of what has been enacted before. Thus everything remains as uncertain and menacing at the end as it was at the beginning. This ambiguity is regarded by some as highly effective, and by others as an artistic flaw. Both Belinsky and Nemirovich-Danchenko consider the Gendarme's appearance and pronouncement to be an essential part of the play, whereas the critic Khrapchenko treats it as an artificial contrivance since 'it is not dictated by the inner development of the action but embodies Gogol's belief in tsarist justice'.[1] Stepanov, another modern critic, agrees that the denouement reflects the author's loyalist outlook, but argues that it does not spoil the play because Gogol has brought about in his spectators a sense of the disparity between the ideal and the real and thus led them to draw the 'right' political conclusions.[2]

A different problem, one of a purely technical nature, is posed by the dumb scene, which represents the moment of truth, illuminating all that has gone before. This elaborately formal tableau, in which the play reaches the point of maximum tension and the effect of which should be shattering, according to Gogol, is notoriously difficult to stage effectively. With the best will in the world, few actors can stand for long like lifeless statues, frozen to the spot. The strain is altogether too great and in practice the curtain generally falls after about 10-15 seconds, although Gogol directed that the scene should last almost $1\frac{1}{2}$ minutes, having already reduced it from 2-3 minutes after seeing the difficulty of sustaining it so long in production. One way of solving this problem is for the producer to modify the scene, as Meyerhold and Ilyinsky did, so that it may run the full length of time without losing its impact. Such a solution, though it violates the letter of Gogol's instructions, accords entirely with their spirit and serves to set a symbolic seal on the entire piece.

The Government Inspector is unrivalled by any other Russian play for its sheer comic power, sustained from beginning to end. In it the comic element, which is predominantly satirical, derives from three sources: situation, character and speech. Comic situations are the least important source of humour. The comic springs are chiefly in the characters themselves, though the play is not a comedy of character in the traditional sense, as applied to Molière's works, for example.

The nub of the plot is a case of mistaken identity which creates a situation of dramatic irony from the beginning of Act II almost to the very end of the play, when the truth comes out. The error opens up comic possibilities which are exploited to the full. The point of maximum comic intensity is attained in the very middle of the play, in Act III, Sc. 5, where the Governor and Zemlyanika vie with each other in self-praise, and Sc. 6, where Khlestakov holds the stage with a spontaneous outpouring of rodomontade. Other comic high points are Act II, Sc. 8, Act IV, Sc. 3-7, and Act V, Sc. 8. Comic confusion is at its best in Act II, Sc. 8, where the Governor first encounters Khlestakov. Much of the time the two protagonists talk at cross-purposes, and a humorously revealing contrast emerges between the words the Governor speaks out loud and his real thoughts, conveyed in asides.

There is a piquant irony in the fact that he swallows Khlestakov's lies but disbelieves him when he tells the truth; the wily old fox is nonplussed by an innocent young puppy.

Physical comedy is used sparingly and for the most part with a purpose, not simply to serve a farcical turn; only in the wooing scenes of Act IV does the play verge on farce, and even then it is with the aim of parodying popular sentimental drama. Thus, when Dr. Hiebner babbles a few incoherent sounds we are given some inkling of the state of Russian medicine at that time, and when the Governor is about to don a hat-box instead of his hat he reveals his state of agitation. Even the antics of Bobchinsky and Dobchinsky are not mere buffoonery, but illustrate their curiosity or anxiety to please. These two droll dumplings are the most innocent people in the play and the only ones who are funny in themselves, yet even they no more strive to amuse than any of the others.

The comedy abounds in sparkling dialogue, punctuated by occasional flashes of wit. It is above all a play of verbal humour expressed in vigorous and varied language, with subtle overtones, many of them quite impossible to capture in English. The stylistic device used most frequently is repetition. This is sometimes employed for other than comic effects; in the opening scenes, for instance, the words 'inspector' and 'incognito' resound like sinister shots, and Khlestakov's repeated use of the patronising remark 'Good' in the second half of Act IV betrays his growing arrogance. But generally the reverberations are humorous, as when Bobchinsky repeats the words with which Dobchinsky interrupts his rambling narrative, appropriating them to himself, or when the Postmaster twice repeats the unflattering description of the Governor given in Khlestakov's letter. A comic boomerang effect is produced by the phrase 'Oh, such goings-on!' (Ах, какой пассаж!) used first by Anna Andreyevna and then by her daughter when each discovers the other being wooed by Khlestakov. In the bribery scenes of Act IV each official uses the same form of words on entering ('I have the honour to introduce myself') and when taking his leave ('I will not presume to intrude on you further'), clasping his sword or bowing as he does so. The repetition of these stock formulae, and similar ones such as 'Quite so, sir' (так точно-с) and 'Not at all, sir' (никак нет-с) tends to diminish the humanity of the people who trot them out to the accompaniment of ritualised gestures, which fit perfectly Bergson's definition of the comic as 'something mechanical encrusted upon the living'. And a similar effect is achieved by Gogol's comparisons, in which human beings are demeaned by being likened to the denizens of the animal kingdom. In Khlestakov's eyes Zemlyanika is a perfect pig in a skull-cap and the Governor as stupid as a grey gelding. To the Governor the wispy Khlestakov in his tail-coat looks just like a fly with its wings clipped, and his description of Bobchinsky and Dobchinsky as bob-tailed magpies is equally apt.

Hyperbole, Gogol's most typical device, is effectively employed by three of the characters. Osip likens the rumblings in his stomach to the roar of a whole regiment of men sounding their bugles and declares that his hunger is so acute that he could devour 'the whole world'. The Governor indicates the remoteness of his provincial town by claiming that it is three years' gallop from any frontier, and later he reproaches the merchants with draining the contents of sixteen samovars a day, such is their addiction to tea. But Khlestakov's exaggerations are the boldest and most far-fetched of all, as befits his character. They reach a climax in the famous bragging scene (III,6), where he speaks of the sumptuous entertainment given at balls in St. Petersburg and cites by way of example a water-melon costing 700 roubles. He arrogates to himself the authorship of various dramatic, operatic and other works, adding casually that he tossed them all off in a single evening. Later he claims that when a temporary replacement was sought for the head of his department he was eventually seen as the only man for the job, whereupon no fewer than 35,000 couriers scoured the city streets in search of him.

Gogol further displays great inventive powers as a creator of verbal inconsequence and nonsense. A classic example of pseudo-explanation occurs early in the play when, in answer to the Governor's complaint that a certain court assessor always reeks of alcohol, the Judge reports the unfortunate man as saying that as a child he was bruised by his nurse and there has been a whiff of vodka about him ever since. Illogicality shows itself again when the Director of Schools is reprimanded for allowing liberal ideas to be instilled into his pupils because one of the teachers pulled faces at them whilst the marshal of the nobility was on a visit. And Anna Andreyevna produces a noteworthy *non sequitur* when she indignantly protests that her eyes must be dark since she always tells her fortune by the queen of clubs.

Absurdity and ineptitude of speech are even commoner than illogicality. The Governor instructs the Postmaster to open other people's letters 'just a little' and read them. Khlestakov seeks to console Anna Andreyevna for living in the remote provinces by pointing out that the country, 'too', has its little hills and brooks. And later she reports him as threatening that if she did not requite his feelings he would put an end to his life 'by dying'. Zemlyanika, during his tête-à-tête with Khlestakov, is told that he appears a little taller than he did the previous day, and the complaisant official replies that it is very likely so, being only too ready to concede an overnight increase in stature in order to please his superior. In Act IV a typically Gogolian exchange takes place when Khlestakov, alone with Maria for the first time, enquires where she was intending to go, and she tells him she was going nowhere. When he demands to know why, her answer is that she thought her mother might be there, but he insists again on knowing why she was 'going nowhere'. Soon after this he proposes to her mother and pledges his instant undying love, but she demurs on the grounds that she is 'in a manner of speaking' already married. He brushes her objection aside and, striving to echo the literary sentimentalists, declaims rhapsodically: 'We shall retreat to the shade of the waters...' – a precious piece of nonsense.

Gogol played a major part in breaking down the barriers between written and spoken Russian, thereby accomplishing the same kind of reform in prose that Pushkin had achieved in verse, and incidentally earning himself much opprobrium for flouting the literary canons of the time by using words and expressions that were not accepted in the beau monde. His dramatic dialogue is predominantly colloquial, but embraces many other styles, the formally polite, the high-flown romantic, the bureaucratic, the commonplace and the crude. Replete with the idioms and rhythms of spoken Russian, it incorporates anacolutha, pleonasms, solecisms, repetitions, hesitations and rhetorical questions – all features of everyday speech. The dialogue is thus natural, yet not naturalistic, for it is not a replica of authentic discourse, but ordinary speech concentrated and raised to the level of art. Gogol's mastery of language and verbal exuberance created dialogue such as had never been heard on the Russian stage before and has seldom been equalled since. His creative, poetic use of the vernacular has been noted by more than one commentator. In 1842 Stepan Shevyrev, a literary critic, wrote of the 'inexhaustible poetry of the play's comic style'[3] and later the famous producer Nemirovich-Danchenko said that he conceived of the play 'as if it were written in verse'. And indeed the work often attains the density of poetic diction, yielding many a pregnant and now proverbial phrase, such as the Governor's remarks 'You take more than your rank allows!', 'She (the N.C.O.'s wife) flogged herself', and Khlestakov's observation that the purpose of life is 'to pluck the flowers of pleasure' – his philosophy in a nutshell.

In the final text of the play, produced after much painstaking revision and refinement, every word and phrase counts and each remark, even the most inconsequential, throws some light on the character of the speaker. Each participant, while remaining faithful to the speech of the time and of his social class, possesses his own manner of speaking; here, in truth, the style proclaims the man. This difference in speech characteristics, largely an innovation in Russian drama,[4] is what brings the fictitious persons to life and stamps them with individuality. It is this gallery of memorable, sharply drawn characters, each with his or her own voice, that makes the comedy as fresh and alive today as when it was written.

The Governor, a petty bureaucratic tyrant and ambitious careerist of small education, is the sharpest and most rapacious as well as the most important of all the officials. He speaks with greater expressiveness and a wider range of tones than anyone else in the play, trimming his tongue to each person and situation he has to deal with. He now rants and bullies, now flatters and fawns. When addressing his colleagues he uses a familiar tone and exerts his authority with ironic politeness. With Khlestakov he is extremely deferential, couching his thoughts in dry officialese and assuming the mask of a loyal, upright guardian of order. With members of his family his speech is unbuttoned, sometimes even coarse and abusive, but he vents his ripest invective on the merchants, whom he believes to have betrayed him. His language is normally racy and colourful, seasoned with expletives, so strong at times that his wife chides him for it. It bespeaks a man of robust instinct, one who professes religion only for reasons of respectability, referring hypocritically to God, sin and Christian duty, while at heart he is a fatalist. He is inclined to deliver himself of gnomic utterances, lapsing on occasion into rhetorical phrases of vacuous orotundity.

Second in importance among the town officials is the Judge, a pompous ass, fond of fornication and hare-coursing, who seeks to give the impression of being a liberal-minded sceptic who thinks for himself. He indulges in homespun philosophy and prides himself on his knowledge, though his reading is paltry and he is deplorably ignorant of the law, like most Russian magistrates at that time. He pontificates ponderously and in booming tones, using short, simple constructions for maximum effect, and although he occasionally resorts to a literary turn of phrase, his style is for the most part formal and undistinguished.

Most devious and sycophantic of the officials is Zemlyanika, a sneak and toady of aldermanic girth. He wheedles and ingratiates himself in unctuous, dulcet tones, posing as a zealous servant of the state and denouncing several of his colleagues behind their backs. It is he who, having suggested that they should bribe Khlestakov and see him individually, contrives to go in last of the officials so that he can tell tales against them without the risk of being informed on himself. His speech, now honeyed and now coarse, matches the duplicity of his character.

Very different is the Postmaster, who is no hypocrite but a simple soul with an insatiable curiosity about other people's doings, which he indulges by prying into the private correspondence that passes through his hands. The least articulate of the officials, he has difficulty in expressing his thoughts and feelings, easily gets tongue-tied or lost for words and speaks in short, broken phrases. His poverty of vocabulary reflects his poverty of spirit.

Khlopov is the official most lacking in personality. He is a timid, mouse-like creature, easily worried by the least thing and absolutely terrified at the prospect of his schools being inspected. He hardly dares to open his mouth for fear of putting his foot in it, and his speech is punctuated with expressions of anxiety and exclamations of alarm.

The fussy little pot-bellied squirelings Bobchinsky and Dobchinsky are figures that derive from the tradition of the *commedia dell'arte*. Yet though they are remarkably alike in appearance, these near-twins are nicely differentiated in character. Bobchinsky, a bachelor, is the sprightlier and more garrulous; Dobchinsky, the family man, is more staid and serious. They are extremely courteous to everyone they meet and share a passion for spreading tales about town. Both gesticulate a great deal and speak rapidly, fearful of being interrupted, liberally sprinkling their speech with particles and interjections. Their sentences are as shapeless and inelegant as they are themselves.

Osip, Khlestakov's manservant, is a dour, canny peasant who has seen much but says little. He is as economical with his tongue as with odd pieces of string or anything else and can sum up a situation in a few apt words. He speaks in an even tone and adopts an insolent, ironic manner towards his master, for whom he has scant respect. His language is that of a domestic serf who has lived long enough in St. Petersburg to acquire a superficial metropolitan veneer and a smattering of city speech. He makes abundant use of affective suffixes, comes out with pseudo-learned coinages such as заботность ('troublesomeness') and mispronounces words of foreign origin in the vernacular fashion, saying *keyatr* for *teatr* ('theatre') and *preshpekt* for *prospekt* ('avenue'). His monologue at the beginning of Act II, a gem of salty, idiomatic and at times ungrammatical Russian, is one of the finest pieces of writing in the whole play. The other servants, the policemen and the petitioners all speak a pure Russian of the people, and Gogol paid careful attention to reproducing the nuances of merchants' speech.

Anna Andreyevna and her daughter are typical women of the provincial gentry. The vain, snobbish mother fancies herself irresistible to men, yearns for life in high society and reveals her pretensions to gentility in her affected use of words and expressions derived from French; the one word амбре ('sweet scent') epitomises her conception of bliss – a scent-laden boudoir, redolent of sensual pleasure. But when rebuking her husband or daughter she soon betrays her essential vulgarity and lapses into an earthier colloquial style. Maria is also flirtatious, but at the same time she is more modest and straightforward than her mother, who is plainly jealous of her. She is an artless, sentimental young lady, lacking in self-assurance. Her speech, bereft of individuality, is the most neutral language used by anyone in the play.

Khlestakov, the principal character, is one of Gogol's greatest creations, a figure worthy to be set beside Shakespeare's Falstaff and Rostand's Cyrano de Bergerac. A junior civil servant from a landowning family of modest means, he represents a new breed of bureaucrat, the young scion of the gentry who is attracted by the glitter of urban life and seeks to ape the grand style of the opulent, even to become a trend-setter. His dominant passion is to show off, to appear important and cultured, but besides being a poseur he is many other things: dandy, philanderer, sensualist, gambler, braggart, fantasist and empty windbag. He is a nullity, but a complex nullity. Whereas the Governor is a purposeful opportunist who actively exploits his position to the utmost, Khlestakov is an aimless opportunist who passively waits on people and events. The Governor's lies are those of a politician, directed towards self-preservation and self-advancement, while Khlestakov's lies are those of the romancer, aimed at self-gratification and self-aggrandisement. He lives wholly in the present, takes his pleasures where he can find them and acts entirely according to the whim of the moment. A shallow, irresponsible egotist, he is too weak to be a convincing villain and too stupid to be a scheming impostor.[5] He is genuinely surprised at the executive-style lunch with which he is regaled at the hospital, not realising that it has been provided to soften him up. In his innocence he never suspects that the banknotes eagerly thrust into his hand by the officials are anything more than loans; he does not know how to take bribes because he is too lowly to have been offered them before. And it is a long time before it dawns on him that he has been taken for an important personage.

In contrast to the local officials, most of whom are ageing, portly and slow of speech, Khlestakov is youthful, slightly built and a rapid speaker. He is all quicksilver, mercurial, with swift changes of front, and his speech mirrors his fluid character. He gabbles jerkily, using disjointed and often unfinished phrases, as his grasshopper mind flits bewilderingly from one subject to another. His tone varies with his mood and his interlocutor. He can be pretentious and arrogant, or craven and conciliatory. Towards servants he is alternately wheedling and abusive; with others he can be polite or familiar, flippant or grave, now mincing, now grovelling, blustering and hectoring by turns and, when he is scared, yelling like a whipped whelp. His speech comprises many elements: colloquial and demotic vocabulary, civil service jargon, card players' slang, salon phrases and snatches of well-known verse; but his style is for the most part neutral and conventional. His comparisons are commonplace, his poetic rhetoric is banal, even his invective is trite. He is at his most inept when seeking to impress the ladies as a gallant by airing the little French he has and uttering phrases of exaggerated politeness, as for example when he enquires of Maria: 'May I dare to be so happy as to offer you a chair?' He is at his best in the bragging scene, where in a state of verbal intoxication he vaunts himself with increasing extravagance in such mega-lomaniac flights of fancy that the officials, already frightened out of their wits, are stunned with awe. Here he is, revelling in the limelight, a Russian Munchausen who transforms lying into a creative art and imposes upon his listeners his own image of himself – commanding, magnificent, omnicompetent.

Various suggestions have been made as to the literary antecedents Gogol may have had in mind when he created his Khlestakov. Among these are famous liars of West European drama such as Dorante in Corneille's *Le Menteur* (1643), Mascarille in Molière's *Les Précieuses ridicules* (1659), Lelio in Goldoni's *Il Bugiardo* (1750), and similar figures in Russian comedy, including Verkholet in Knyazhnin's *The Braggart* (1786), Semyon in Krylov's *Lesson to the Daughters* (1807), Alnaskarov in Khmelnitsky's *Castles in the Air* (1818), and Pustolobov in Kvitka's *Visitor from the Capital* (written 1827). Similarities certainly exist between Khlestakov and these other stage liars, but there is a very important difference that marks him off from them. Gogol's hero is no deliberate deceiver; he lies without intending to delude other people, seeking only to impress them. In this respect he represents a significant transformation of the traditional figure of the impostor. To create a new, passive type of hero who stumbles into the role of a 'great man' was in fact a stroke of genius on Gogol's part.

There has been much conjecture, too, about possible prototypes of Khlestakov from among Gogol's contemporaries, understandably so since the Russian theatre, from the time of Catherine, had presented comedies with characters based on, and usually satirising, living persons – the so-called комедии на лица.[6] Nikolai Sazonov, a prominent Russian emigré in Paris, confidently asserted in an anonymously published work that *The Government Inspector* was a political lampoon, the hero of which was none other than the Emperor himself, transformed into a petty official.[7] It is tempting to see Nicholas I, who frequently made tours of inspection in his empire, as a model for Khlestakov. However, quite apart from the total dissimiliarity in appearance and character between the two men, the claim is untenable in view of the deep reverence Gogol is known to have always had for the person of the Tsar. Satirist though he was, Gogol would have drawn the line at ridiculing the monarch, who for him was sacrosanct.

Much more plausible as Khlestakov's original is the journalist Pavel Svinyin, a notorious liar who figured in one of the anecdotes Pushkin is reported to have told Gogol and who is also known to have inspired Zarnitskin in Shakhovskoi's *Don't listen if you don't like it* (1818). Svinyin is probably also the true identity of a certain 'Radugin', the Muscovite notability who is shown in the literary supplement to *The Russian Invalid* (No. 83, 1834) boasting to Saratov provincials of his high position and esteem in both capitals. Gogol attended at-homes given by the paper's editor A. Voyeikov and could well have met Svinyin at such gatherings.[8]

Tikhonravov, who produced the first scholarly edition of Gogol's works, saw a resemblance between Khlestakov and another contemporary journalist, Faddei Bulgarin. It is true that Bulgarin was an irrepressible braggart who laid claim to great literary talent and friendship with eminent writers, but Gogol clearly did not have him in mind when creating Khlestakov because in the first two versions of the play the hero actually boasts of dining with Bulgarin.[9]

Two scholars, V. Gippius and A. S. Dolinin, have proposed as Khlestakov's prototype Bulgarin's equally bumptious colleague Osip Senkovsky.[10] Gogol heartily disliked the indefatigable editor of *The Library for Reading*, whose brand of journalism he roundly condemned in an article of 1836, and he ridicules him in Act III, Sc. 6, where Khlestakov claims to be Baron Brambeus (a pseudonym used by Senkovsky), boasts of his fecundity as a writer and of his princely salary, adding that he corrects everyone's articles. It should be noted, however, that this forms only a small part of one scene, touching Khlestakov the would-be writer, and even then he claims the authorship of other works besides those of Senkovsky.

The evidence suggests that Gogol had Senkovsky in mind, partly at least, and possibly Svinyin too, when creating the character of Khlestakov, but he had a more immediate source of inspiration, namely himself. There seems no doubt that, consciously or unconsciously, he put a good deal of himself into his Khlestakov, for the resemblances are too striking to be ignored. Petty vanity, shameless mendacity, a desire to impress, even the habit of borrowing money – all these Khlestakovian traits were part of Gogol's complex make-up. Like his hero, Gogol was vain about his appearance, indeed the foppish tendency that was quite marked in him as a young man re-emerged occasionally even in his later years. Khlestakov's salient characteristic, as Gogol observed in a letter to Sosnitsky dated 2 November 1846, is his 'sincere desire to act the part of someone with a rank higher than his own'. Such was Gogol's own behaviour in 1832 when, according to Annenkov, he altered the rank in his travel document from collegiate registrar (14th grade) to collegiate assessor (8th grade) so that he should be mentioned in the *Moscow News*, which printed the names of all persons entering or leaving the city who possessed the eighth or a higher rank.

Gogol displayed a Khlestakov-like arrogance when he set out to conquer the academic world by proclaiming it his intention to write a history of the Ukraine in four to six volumes, a history of the Middle Ages in eight to nine volumes, and a history of the world in ten volumes, each of them, like the loans Khlestakov requests, larger than the one before. He accepted a post at St. Petersburg University and cast himself in the role of a great historian who, once armed with an extensive knowledge of the past, would be able to divine the future and even presume to advise the Tsar. And he revealed a breathtaking combination of presumptuousness and naivety, akin to Khlestakov's, in expecting *The Government Inspector* to bring about a magical revolution in the morals of his people, something no other Russian writer had ever dared to attempt.

In his later years Gogol's Khlestakovism took a spiritual turn as he became firmly convinced that he was a chosen instrument of God's will. His acts of philanthropy were performed ostentatiously, in flagrant contradiction to the humility he preached so earnestly. His letters to relatives and friends contained lofty moral advice expressed in an authoritative tone. He was bluntly rebuked by Sergei Aksakov for parading his piety and for his sermonising, 'full of pride clothed in the ragged garb of humility'. The same priggish manner mars those letters in *Selected Passages* in which he sets himself up as a prophet and saviour of his generation, showing the light to his benighted countrymen. When abuse was heaped upon him for his pains he realised that he had gone too far, that his preacherly tone had been a mistake.

In a letter to Zhukovsky, written shortly after the book appeared, he described the effect it had produced as a slap in the face for the public, his

friends, and most of all himself. 'After its publication,' he wrote, 'I came to
. my senses, just as if I had come out of some dream, feeling, like a guilty
schoolboy, that I had done more mischief than I intended. In my book I made
an exhibition of myself in such a Khlestakovian fashion that I have not the
courage to look at it...How ashamed I am of myself...Truly, there is something Khlestakovian about me.' This confession amply confirmed the truth
of his earlier observation, made in his *Extract from a Letter*, that there is
something of Khlestakov in nearly all of us. 'Your smart[11] Guards officer
sometimes proves to be a Khlestakov;' he wrote, 'your statesman sometimes
proves a Khlestakov, and we literary men, sinners that we are, at times turn
out to be Khlestakovs.' Small wonder that when he suggested to Aksakov
in 1839 that they should put on an amateur performance of *The Government
Inspector* Gogol chose the part of Khlestakov for himself.

Khlestakov undoubtedly embodies some of his creator's character.
Gogol endowed his hero with the frivolous, superficial aspect of his many-
sided nature, just as he later transferred his own faults, real or imagined, to
the fictional characters in his *Dead Souls*. If this was done consciously, and
Gogol was a more conscious artist than many critics have supposed, then
clearly, in part at least, he was indulging in an act of ironic self-mockery, and
to that extent realising the ideal he later proclaimed, at the end of his
Supplement to The Denouement, that the noblest kind of laughter is
directed at oneself. But Khlestakov should not be seen as a self-portrait on
Gogol's part, for he resembles his creator only in certain respects and not at
all in others.

It is a mistake, in fact, to look for a single prototype, since the assumption
that there was one living original conflicts both with what Gogol wrote of
Khlestakov in particular and with what he tells us of his method of creating
character in general. In his *Extract from a Letter* he describes Khlestakov
as a type that combines diverse features found in Russians of very different
character: what is true of Khlestakov applies to his other literary creations
too. He reveals his method of character-drawing when he states in his
Confession: 'I have never *painted* a portrait in the sense of making a simple
copy. I would *create* a portrait, but create it as a result of deliberation, not out
of my imagination.' In other words, his characters are not pure inventions
but were drawn from reality, without being slavish copies of individuals. Like
Turgenev's characters, they are composite figures, an amalgam of features
taken from various living persons; and although they were not invented, they
were nevertheless built up and worked upon by his creative imagination.

This raises the vexed question of verisimilitude. Does Gogol's method
of creating character produce figures that are lifeless bundles of characteristics, distorted creatures with human attributes, or recognizably real
people? Ever since the time when *The Government Inspector* first appeared
critical opinion has been sharply divided on this issue. Nikolai Polevoi, writing

in 1842, referred to Gogol's *dramatis personae* as 'ugly grotesques' and 'figures from a galanty show' (китайские тени).[12] On the other hand, Belinsky described them a year later as 'people, not puppets', with characters that were 'drawn from the innermost recesses of Russian life'.[13] Over a century later critics still view his dramatic characters very differently. A. Anikst writes that the people in Gogol's comedies are 'not caricatures, not grotesque figures, but well-rounded characters taken from the heart of life'.[14] By contrast, D. Mirsky takes the view that Gogol's creatures are 'not realistic caricatures of the world without, but introspective caricatures of the fauna of his own mind', while allowing that those in *The Government Inspector* are 'more supple and human' and 'more ordinary, more average' than those in *Dead Souls*.[15] For V. Erlich the world of *The Government Inspector* is 'populated by homunculi rather than by full-blown human beings, by puppets whose precariously contrived mode of existence is pointed up by their blatantly comic names'.[16]

This divergence of opinion is less perplexing than at first appears. The chief point of disagreement here is that some critics see Gogol's dramatic characters as human, and others see them as grotesque: the fact is that there is some truth in both assessments. Belinsky was right in saying that the characters are not puppets, since they are no more marionettes than they are embodiments of a particular passion or idea, as were the characters of traditional comedy. But Belinsky was wrong in seeing them as absolutely real, flesh-and-blood people, for they are not fully rounded human characters such as one finds, for example, in Chekhov's plays or Tolstoy's novels. There is an element of caricature in Gogol's portrayal, as there must be in satire. He accentuates salient features in his characters, just as he magnifies their verbal idiosyncrasies. He uses the technique of intensification, of meticulously individualised caricature, to achieve his artistic purpose; only by a measure of exaggeration could his satirical point be made strongly enough to strike home with his audience. Yet his dramatic characters are not so overdrawn as to lose their credibility as human beings and become merely comic or grotesque masks. They are not the simple caricatures of farce, but still recognisable as people, though many are larger than life.

Gogol condemned the lay figures of melodrama and farce, and sought to create complex stage characters with varied and sometimes contradictory traits who were convincing as people. His belief that he had succeeded in this is expressed in *Leaving the Theatre* by one of his mouthpieces, the Second Spectator, who observes that the impression left by the play 'is all the stronger for the fact that none of the persons in it has lost his human image: the human is apparent everywhere'.

The characters of Gogol's comedy are moulded in the common clay of humanity. Even the least of them, who appear but briefly or not at all in the flesh – those fleeting figures on the fringes of the action – seem fully alive.

They none of them resemble the grotesque creations of E.T.A. Hoffmann or Edgar Allan Poe. They are not monsters of ugliness or depravity; on the contrary, they are ordinary people and the officials, though rogues, are good-natured rogues with redeeming virtues. The degree of exaggeration in their portrayal is not such as to warrant speaking of them as grotesque, for the mark of the grotesque is that it grossly distorts nature, rendering it weird, alien and inhuman.[17]

There are genuine touches of verbal grotesque in *The Government Inspector*, but Gogol's caricature in the portrayal of the people in his play is not pushed to a grotesque extreme and does not destroy their essential humanity. His caricature is mild, just as his satire is gentle, even sympathetic, and not of the same order as the savage satire of a Swift or a Voltaire. Moreover, Gogol's figures are unmistakably human types and this would not be so if they were grotesquely drawn, since the grotesque is wholly individual and never typical. The names of many characters in the play have become by-words among Russians. And they are not only types belonging to their own class and period; they are universal types found in many kinds of society, in conditions quite different from those prevailing in the Russia of Gogol's time.

Just as the characters in *The Government Inspector* are often erroneously called grotesque, so is the town in which it is set sometimes described as queer and the whole world of the play as unreal, abnormal, even mad.[18] There is certainly some truth in these descriptions, but it is greatly exaggerated. The town, like its inhabitants, is not wholly real, but it is not so very different from real Russian towns of that time. Gogol made clear, again through the Second Spectator in *Leaving the Theatre*, that he was presenting a composite image of a typical provincial town, in the same way as he produced composite and typical characters to people it. His town differs from real ones only in that it is run by none but corrupt administrators; this was an exaggeration, but not a great exaggeration, at least in Russia under Nicholas I. Again, the words and behaviour of the characters are odd and illogical, but only part of the time, only a little more often than one finds in real life; they are not to be compared with the ramblings and erratic acts of lunatics. The play would not have had the impact we know it had on Gogol's contemporaries if the town and its inhabitants had not been close enough to life to be recognised. The truth is that the world presented here is not far removed from reality. If it is 'abnormal' or 'mad', then its abnormality and madness are those of the ordinary world, not the world of pathology.[19]

Because much of Gogol's fiction takes us into the world of the grotesque, the fantastic and the absurd, it has been assumed, far too readily, that these are the dominant traits of everything he created. To be sure, there is an affinity between all his writings, but the hyperbolism inherent in Gogol's imagination manifests itself in very different degrees in his various works. *The Government Inspector* is not the same as *The Nose, Viy, The Memoirs of a Madman* or even *Dead Souls*, the work to which it stands closest. Nor, though it contains elements of the absurd, does it belong to the absurdist drama. While it deviates from literal truth to life, the play remains by and large 'realistic', though Gogol's literary manner cannot be adequately described by this or any other single term, however widely defined. No man, least of all a great artist, can be captured in one word.

Interpretation and Significance

The Government Inspector is remarkable as a drama in uniting very different, seemingly incongruous elements and styles in one harmonious whole. It combines surface gaiety with hidden horror, ranging from farce at one extreme to tragedy at the other. It mingles laughter with tears, the literal with the symbolical, the trivial with the profound. It is at once absurdly frivolous and deeply serious. Its style ranges from the highly formal to the lowly informal. This unique blend of qualities makes it difficult to classify the play within any of the recognised dramatic genres. It may be best described, perhaps, as a satirical comedy of confusion and corruption.

The human problem on which Gogol focusses his attention in the play is that of bribery, a practice which had become institutionalised in Russia well before the age of Nicholas I. It had evolved an elaborate code, in which a distinction was made between 'innocent income' (безгрешные доходы), derived from private persons, and 'sinful income' (грешные доходы), acquired at the expense of the state. It was considered tactful to suborn indirectly and to avoid referring to the bribe as such, using instead various euphemisms, such as 'a lamb wrapped in paper' (барашек в бумажке). Gogol had observed bribery at first hand during his time in the civil service and came to deplore it as a grave social evil. At the time he wrote his play he believed that bribery could be banished, or at least diminished, by being ridiculed on the stage. Through his satire he was appealing to the conscience of Russian officials, reminding them of their duty to the state and urging them to mend their ways, but his plea fell on deaf ears. He overestimated the power of mockery and underestimated the force of habit. More conducive to probity in office are the payment of adequate salaries, open government and continual vigilance on the part of the authorities. But legislative and administrative mechanisms, helpful though they are, cannot of themselves ensure rectitude in the management of public affairs; in the last analysis this depends on the character of the officials and negotiators themselves. The truth of this is shown by the fact that no social system has succeeded in eliminating corruption from the conduct of administration or business, though the corruption is more rife in some countries, where it is sanctioned by custom, than in others, where it is condemned by public opinion. Gogol's play is thus as relevant to the world of the twentieth century as it was to its own time, and it points to a perennial evil of civilised societies.

Yet, when all is said and done, *The Government Inspector* is not simply, nor even primarily, an indictment of bribery or a satire on bureaucratic corruption and incompetence, any more than it is merely a comedy of mistaken identity. It has much wider implications, for there is always more in Gogol than meets the eye. At a deeper level it can be seen as an attack on all forms of moral depravity, of which bribery and corruption are but examples. Many other abuses are to be found in Gogol's town: beating, torture, lying, informing, misappropriation of funds, falsification of returns and interference with private mail. Besides these forms of bureaucratic oppression and injustice many vices are exhibited, among them hypocrisy, vanity, snobbery, acquisitiveness, place-seeking and love of power.

Particularly evident is that vice which in Russian goes by the name of *poshlost'*, a combination of smug vulgarity and pettiness of soul. It was Pushkin who first noted Gogol's exceptional flair for portraying the quality of *poshlost'* in people, and this gift is nowhere more vividly displayed than in *The Government Inspector*. What Gogol gives us here is a set of variations on the theme of *poshlost'*, with each of the characters shown as vulgar in his or her own way. Khlestakov himself is the embodiment of a particular kind of *poshlost'*, of a mental and spiritual vacuity allied to airy fantasising about a life of fame and luxury; and he carries the others away on the troika of his imagination, inspiring them to indulge in similar fantasies. The Governor dreams of obtaining high rank and decorations; his wife fancies herself mistress of the finest house in all St. Petersburg; Dobchinsky conjures up a picture of the rich clothes Maria will wear there and the rare soups of which she will partake. The *poshlost'* assumes many guises, but always represents the commonplace core of corruption. In this way *The Government Inspector* demonstrates, as perhaps no other work of literature has done, the banality of evil and the evil of banality.

The real object of Gogol's wide-ranging satire is thus not any specific abuse, such as bribery, or particular vice, such as hypocrisy, but moral corruption as such, of which *poshlost'* is the most insidious and ubiquitous form. In Gogol's eyes most men were sunk in a morass of futile triviality, living lives of grey mediocrity in a state of spiritual sloth, prisoners of their own prejudices, passions and possessions. It was against this deadness of soul, this pervasive *poshlost'* that he wrestled constantly in his writings, for he had a horror of the void, especially the void inside man himself. He had perceived that the death in life is far more terrible than the death after life.

None of the characters in *The Government Inspector* gives anything more than a conventional nod in the direction of things of the mind or spirit. When Khlestakov expresses a wish for 'spiritual nourishment', he is merely aping those with lofty ideals and presenting a pathetic caricature of Gogol's own aspirations; and when he declares that his 'soul thirsts for culture' this turns out to be as much a travesty of real culture as his wooing is a parody of true romance. The Governor, a man ambitious for advancement, assures Khlestakov that he seeks no honours since 'beside virtue all else is dust and ashes', a remark that epitomises his hypocrisy. The Judge, who is the would-be intellectual among the officials, alludes to what he mistakenly believes is a Masonic book, but this local Cicero is quite unable to make head or tail of court reports and is most at home discoursing on the merits of hunting-dogs. Khlopov, fearful lest the pupils in his schools should imbibe any subversive – that is to say, liberal – ideas, is too diffident to vouchsafe an opinion about anything. The Postmaster has not a single idea in his head and would be incapable of articulating it if he had. Anna exclaims to Khlestakov 'How nice it must be to be a writer!' and Maria asks him to inscribe a verse or two in her autograph book, but most of their mental energy is expended in constant bickering about trivial matters, such as which dress each of them is going to wear. This being the intellectual and moral level of the participants, there is great symbolic truth in the final scene of the play, where the townspeople, struck dumb and motionless, reveal their state of living death in a moment of dramatic *rigor mortis*.

Thus, beneath all the humour and gaiety of the play lurks a disturbing sense of the malaise that afflicts all the people in it. They are funny and ridiculous, but they are also hollow, selfish creatures and the corruption in them, though petty, is frightening, the more so because they are such ordinary people. Gogol's view of life, though comic on the surface, is essentially pessimistic. He saw it, to quote his own words in *Dead Souls*, 'through the laughter visible to the world and the tears invisible and unknown to it'. The laughter from which *The Government Inspector* sprang was not a cruel laughter, born of malice, but a cleansing, liberating laughter mingled with tears of sadness and compassion for these morally underdeveloped people living such a mean, empty existence, heedless of all that gives life real meaning. There was at that time no rancour or venom in Gogol's satire. His laughter turned bitter and the iron entered his soul only later, while he was writing the first part of his great novel.[20]

Although the plot of *The Government Inspector* is based on the traditional theme of mistaken identity, Gogol, unlike previous dramatists who had used this device, exploited the error of judgement from which the action unfolds not simply or solely for comic effect, but to reveal a fundamental state of chaos in human life. He abhorred the disorder, especially the moral disorder, he perceived around him and considered the world to be out of joint. It is no accident that the plot of most of his works hinges on a deception, because for him deception was at the very heart of things. He saw human beings as enmeshed in a web of confusion and deceptions, misled not only by appearances but also by their own delusions and lies.

The problem of corruption afforded great scope for exploring in *The Government Inspector* his central theme of deception. The confusion and misunderstandings that abound in the play testify to the perils and pitfalls of speech, to the malignant power of rumour and gossip. The Governor's remark that 'words do no harm' is richly ironic in the context of a play which demonstrates with striking examples that words do indeed cause great mischief among men and can be their undoing. Words are not as innocent as they seem, just as nothing in the world is, to Gogol, what it seems. Words can conceal our thoughts as well as reveal them, a fact amply illustrated in the play, whose dialogue becomes at times a series of juxtaposed monologues. Finally speech itself proves inadequate, being replaced by the silent language of frozen gestures; and although the mistake concerning the inspector is cleared up, nevertheless confusion still reigns at the end of the play. In purely dramatic terms a denouement is effected, but there is no real resolution, no true end. The situation is that of a vicious circle in which the action has returned to its starting-point.

Seeking an explanation for the error made by the officials, Zemlyanika lights on the devil. 'How it came about, for the life of me I cannot explain,' he says. 'It is as though we were stupefied by some kind of fog, beguiled by the devil.' It is naturally the devil that spreads the fog of cosmic confusion. Shortcomings soon find scapegoats, the most favoured of such goats being the devil and fate; but the true causes of the error and confusion in *The Government Inspector* are plain fear and stupidity, not supernatural forces. Fear, induced by bad consciences, fills the hearts of the officials throughout the play and motivates their behaviour. Gogol shows us what happens when fear dominates men's lives: fear breeds suspicion, deceit and, not least, self-deception. When taxed with having presented no positive characters in his play, Gogol pointed to laughter. In a similar way fear may be personified as a negative character in the work. The fear represents the serious, inner aspect of the play, just as the laughter expresses its external, comic aspect. The laughter and gaiety are on the outside, enjoyed by the spectator, not by the participants themselves; for them it is all deadly earnest since their situation is fraught with danger.

Fear is reinforced by stupidity. Khlestakov succeeds in his ephemeral role because he is too stupid to realise the dangerous situation he is in and because Bobchinsky and Dobchinsky, those virtuosos of topsy-turvy logic, insist that he is the inspector, deducing this from the fact that he had looked at the food on their plates at the inn. The Governor, who is by no means a fool, acts stupidly at a critical moment not only out of fear but because he is simply unable to believe that Khlestakov is really as stupid as he appears to be. The Governor is a victim of his own shrewdness, proving too clever by half and demonstrating the truth of his own dictum that 'in some cases a lot of brains is worse than none at all'. Sceptical of his adversary's claims and inclined at first to disbelieve his story, the Governor stills his own doubts with various more or less satisfactory explanations. He is prepared to accept that Khlestakov may have embroidered a little, for 'there is no speech without a little embroidering', but most of what the young visitor says must be true. Then, after the truth is known, the Governor in a passionate outburst reproaches himself with being blind and mad, but worst of all, stupid. In the end he and his fellow-officials are not punished for their misdemeanours, but instead ridiculed for their folly. The essence of their folly is that they have taken a foolish nonentity for a clever person of importance. And Khlestakov, the nobody, is the victor since he escapes scot-free. Gogol dismayed and disoriented his contemporaries by going against the general rule of comedy whereby poetic justice should prevail, that is to say vice should be punished and virtue rewarded. Indeed, he had offended doubly by leaving out virtue and by failing to ensure that the miscreants are brought to book.

Thus it is not justice, much less virtue, that is seen to triumph in *The Government Inspector*, but rather human folly. The notion of justice is not given concrete shape, for the real inspector is a remote, insubstantial figure who remains behind the scenes, necessarily so, since his appearance on stage would have conflicted with the author's intention that the work should directly depict only what is negative or bad. Yet the real inspector was originally conceived by Gogol as the agent of retribution, the arm of secular justice, and subsequently reinterpreted, in *The Denouement*, as the symbol of divine justice. This later gloss may have been suggested by Belinsky's description of Khlestakov, in his assumed role, as a phantom or shadow of the Governor's bad conscience. To Belinsky the uneasy conscience of the Governor and his associates served simply to explain Khlestakov's easy success, but Gogol took this idea and extended it, transforming the false inspector into man's worldly conscience and the real inspector into man's true conscience, answerable only to God; by this means he linked it with the question of divine judgement. And in making the town symbolise the human soul he doubtless drew on his reading of works by churchmen, for the city-soul is an image found in medieval theology, most notably in St. Augustine's *De Civitate Dei*. The suggestion that the officials of the town represent various human passions was Gogol's own elaboration of the metaphor.

In essence, Gogol's allegorical exegesis propounds the view that man may be arraigned for his crimes by a human judge, but for his corruption or sins of the spirit he can be called to account only by the Supreme Judge. The play, seen in this light, is a salutary reminder of God's all-seeing eye and of the real sense in which we are all in this world on trial for our lives. Its author seems to be asking us, the spectators and readers, whether our lives could stand the test of an inspection, and reminding us that we are as much involved in the action of his play as the participants, because we are all capable of straying and likely to be deceived. We sit in judgement on those participants, but one that is higher than us sits in judgement on us in turn. The notion of God as a 'higher inspector' finds expression in a letter Gogol wrote to Alexandra Smirnova on 6 December 1849, where he says: 'We find it hard, very hard, we who forget at every moment that our actions will be inspected not by some senator, but by Him who cannot be suborned.'

As we know, this symbolic interpretation of *The Government Inspector* was imposed on the play retrospectively and formed no part of the original conception, in which justice was seen solely in secular terms. Gogol, in his mystical period, sought to allegorise his comedy in order to counteract the political meaning that most people had read into it. If his contemporaries could not understand it as the victory of secular justice that he had intended, then he would make them see it in terms of divine justice by removing it from the sphere of the literal altogether. Now it would be wrong to dismiss Gogol's religious symbolism out of hand. After all his play is, at the deepest level, a drama of corruption and judgement in which there reverberates the language of religion – 'miracle', 'faith', 'sin', 'God' and 'the devil'. It is a challenge to the consciences of all who watch it. But the allegorical frame-work in which Gogol tried to fit it is too schematic and restrictive to be satisfactory, particularly when the play is given in the theatre. Shchepkin was right to object that Gogol's attempt to turn the town and the main characters into symbols drained most of the life out of a dramatic work that pulsated with vitality and human interest. It is neither a parable nor a morality play, but first and foremost a drama of real life and real people. Gogol had too great an understanding of the theatre and too much respect for Shchepkin not to see that the great actor was right. In the end, therefore, he decided not to insist on his revised interpretation and was content to place his play, as he did by implication in his *Selected Passages*, in the tradition of social comedy established by Fonvizin and Griboyedov. In building upon that tradition he had revolutionised the theatre in Russia, though he had failed in his purpose of revolutionising Russian morals.

To conclude, *The Government Inspector* is a work of enormous scale, at one extreme an entertaining comedy of errors and, at the other, an illuminating drama of corruption. No single interpretation encompasses all its meaning; it may be understood and appreciated at several different levels – the anecdotal, the satirical, and the metaphysical. It is a play of great originality, that contains the inexhaustible riches of all great art. Its theme is universal and it speaks to the eternal human condition. Its laughter is directed at what is essential and permanent in man. It transcends its own time and people, belonging to all ages and all peoples. It has justly earned for itself the name of immortal comedy.

Notes to Part Two

1. M.B. Khrapchenko, *Творчество Гоголя*, 1954, p. 170.

2. N.L. Stepanov, *Н.В. Гоголь. Творческий путь*, 1955, p. 361.

3. In 1836 Shevyrev, then the regular critic of the Moscow Observer had refused to write a review of *The Government Inspector*, describing it, according to Belinsky, as 'a sordid comedy'; but Gogol and Shevyrev became close friends in 1839.

4. Before Gogol only Fonvizin had individualised his dramatic characters through their speech, and then not fully.

5. D. Merezhkovsky, in his *Гоголь и черт*, Moscow, 1906, p. 10, describes Khlestakov as intelligent. He evidently misread the passage in *Extract from a Letter* (to Pushkin) where Gogol says that the leading role would have been better played if he had given it to one of the least talented actors and told him that the hero was 'cunning, perfectly proper, clever and perhaps even virtuous'. The truth is, of course, that Khlestakov is none of these things, but 'plain stupid', as Gogol states in his letter to Shchepkin of 10 May, 1836. Nor is Osip a fool, as Merezhkovsky says (p. 9), but a shrewd fellow, much sharper than Khlestakov.

6. See D.J. Welsh, *Russian Comedy, 1765-1823*, The Hague, 1966, pp. 19-27.

7. *La vérité sur l'empereur Nicolas*, Paris, 1854, p. 193.

8. See L.V. Krestova, *Комментарий к комедии Н.В. Гоголя "Ревизор"*, Moscow, 1933, p. 100, and N.L. Brodsky, *Избранные труды*, Moscow, 1964, pp. 66-7.

9. E. Voitolovskaya in her *Комментарий*, pp. 194-5, suggests that something of Bulgarin may have gone into the character of Zemlyanika, but there is no resemblance beyond the fact that both were informers (Bulgarin was exposed as such in Pushkin's squib *О записках Видока*, 1830).

10. V.V. Gippius, 'Заметки о Гоголе. III. Вариант Хлестакова', *Ученые записки Ленинградского университета, серия филологических наук*, 1941, Vol. 76, No. 11, p. 10; A.S. Dolinin, 'Из истории борьбы Гоголя и Белинского за идейность в литературе', *Ученые записки Ленинградского гос. пед. института*, 1956, Vol. 18, No. 5, p. 40.

11. Gogol here uses the word ловкий in one of its Ukrainian, not Russian senses.

12. *Русский вестник*, 1842, Vol. 5, No. 1, p. 61.

13. *Отечественные записки*, 1843. See V.G. Belinsky, *Полное собрание сочинений*, Moscow, Vol.7 (1955), p. 85.

14. A. Anikst, *Теория драмы в России от Пушкина до Чехова*, Moscow, 1972, p. 126.

15. D.S. Mirsky, *A History of Russian Literature*, London, 1968, pp. 146, 154.

16. V. Erlich, *Gogol*, New Haven and London, 1969, p. 103.

17. There is no exaggeration at all in some of the portraits, for example those of Osip, Anna and Maria.

18. See, for example, V. Bryusov, *Испепеленный*, Moscow, 1909, p. 14; S. Mashinsky, *Художественный мир Гоголя*, Moscow, 1971, pp. 253-4, p. 258; and W. Harrison's edition of the play, Bradda Books, Letchworth, 1964, pp. 9 & 12.

19. V. Nabokov is mistaken in saying that the comedy has no connection with reality and calling it a 'dream play', whose characters are the kind of people one meets in a nightmare (*Nikolai Gogol*, Norfolk, Connecticut, 1944, pp. 41-2 & p. 54). Curiously enough, Nabokov and Belinsky, whose views of the play are in all other respects diametrically opposed, both failed to recognise it as a moral satire, being misled by the fact that it is not explicitly didactic.

20. This is shown by A. Tertz (pen-name of Andrei Sinyavsky) in his *В тени Гоголя*, London, 1975, pp. 303-20. It is quite untrue to say of the play, as J. Lavrin does in his introduction to D.J. Campbell's translation, p. 9, that 'the laughter which permeates it is hardly less cruel and lashing than that in *Dead Souls*'.

Bibliography

Primary Sources

Beresford, M. (ed.), *N.V. Gogol's Ревизор (The Government Inspector): A Comedy in Five Acts*, The Edwin Mellen Press, Lewiston/Queenston/Lampeter, 1996.
Chulkov, S. (ed.), *Н..В. Гоголь, Сочинения в двух томах. Государственное издательство художественной литературы*, Moscow, 1959, Vol. 2.
Harrison, W., *Gogol: The Government Inspector*, BCP, London, 1992.
Tomashevsky, B.V., *Н.В. Гоголь, Полное собрание сочинений*, Издательство Академии наук СССР, Moscow & Leningrad, 1937-52, Vol. IV.

Studies of Gogol in English

Erlich, V. *Gogol*. New Haven & London, 1969.
Fanger, D. *The Creation of Nikolai Gogol*. Harvard U.P., 1979.
Gippius, V. V. *Gogol*. Ann Arbor, Michigan, 1981. (Russian original pub. Leningrad, 1924.)
Karlinsky, S. *The Sexual Labyrinth of Nikolai Gogol*. Harvard U.P., 1976.
Lavrin, J. *Gogol*. London & New York, 1926, and *Nikolai Gogol (1809-1852). A Centenary Survey*. London, 1951.
Lindstrom, T. S. *Nikolay Gogol*. New York, 1974.
Magarshack, D. *Gogol: A Life*. London & New York, 1957.
Nabokov, V. *Nikolai Gogol*. Norfolk, Connecticut, 1944.
Peace, R. *The Enigma of Gogol*. Cambridge U.P., 1981.
Rowe, W. W. *Through Gogol's Looking Glass*. New York U.P., 1976.
Setchkarev, V. *Gogol: His Life and Works*. London & New York, 1965. (German original pub. Wiesbaden & Berlin, 1953.)
Troyat, H. *Divided Soul: The Life of Gogol*. New York, 1973.(French original pub. Paris, 1971.)
Zeldin, J. *Nikolai Gogol's Quest for Beauty*. Regents Press of Kansas, 1978.

Gogol's dramatic works

Anikst, A. A. 'Гоголь о реализме в драме', *Театр*, 3 (1952), 41-52.
Anikst, A. A. 'Н. В. Гоголь о драме', in his *Теория драмы в России от Пушкина до Чехова*. Moscow, 1972, 106-31.
Danilov, S. S. *Гоголь и театр*. Leningrad, 1936.
Dokusov, A. M. *Драматургия Н. В. Гоголя*. Leningrad, 1962.
Durylin, S. N. 'Гоголь и театр', *Бюллетень АН, серия истории и философии*, IX/2 (1952), 144-64.
Durylin, S. N. 'От «Владимира третьей степени» к «Ревизору»', in *Ежегодник Института истории искусств*, Moscow, 1953, 164-239.
Gorbulina, E. V. 'Литературно-критическая борьба вокруг драматургии Н. В. Гоголя в 30–40-х годах XIX в.', *Ученые записки Ворошиловского пед. института, серия историко-филологических наук*, т.XXIV, вып.1 (1957), 67-116.
Gourfinkel, N. 'Gogol et le théâtre', *Revue d'histoire du théâtre*, 3 (1952), 189-219.
Gourfinkel, N. *Nicolas Gogol, dramaturge*. Paris, 1956.
Khrapchenko, M. B. 'Драматургия Гоголя', *Октябрь*, 1 (1952), 141-74.
Kremlev, A. N. 'Драматические произведения Гоголя и взгляды его на значение театра', *Образование*, 4 (1909), 42-59.
Kryzhitsky, G. 'О драматургии Гоголя', *Театр*, 12 (1952), 114-18.
Kupreyanova, E. N. 'Гоголь-комедиограф', *Русская литература*, 1 (1990), 6-33.
Mann, Yu. V. 'Парадокс Гоголя-драматурга', *Вопросы литературы*, 12 (1981), 132-47.
Matskin, A. P. *На темы Гоголя: Театральные очерки*. Moscow, 1984.
Nemirovich-Danchenko, V. I. 'Тайны сценического обаяния Гоголя', *Ежегодник императорских театров*, вып.2 (1909), 28-35.
Pfulb, A. 'Comment Gogol concevait le théâtre', *La Pensée. Nouvelle série*, 44 (1952), 105-10.
Piksanov, N. K. *Гоголь-драматург. Стенограмма публичной лекции*. Leningrad, 1952.

Pokusayev, E. I. 'Гоголь об «истинно общественной» комедии', *Русская литература*, 2 (1959), 31–44.
Romashov, B. S. 'Великий художник русского театра', *Театр*, 3 (1952), 3–17.
Rozanov, V. V. 'Гоголь и его значение для театра', in his *Среди художников*, St. Petersburg, 1914, 264–71.
Stepanov, N. L. (Ed.) *Гоголь и театр*. Moscow, 1952.
Stepanov, N. L. *Искусство Гоголя-драматурга*. Moscow, 1964.
Thiess, F. *Nikolaus W. Gogol und seine Bühnenwerke*. Berlin, 1922.
Varneke, B. V. 'Гоголь и театр', *Русский филологический вестник*, 2 (1909), 307–36.
Vishnevskaya, I. L. *Гоголь и его комедии*. Moscow, 1976.
Volkova, L. P. '«Русский чисто анекдот» — структурообразующий принцип гоголевской драматургии', *Вопросы русской литературы*, 55 (1990), 3–12.
Worrall, N. *Nikolai Gogol and Ivan Turgenev*. London, 1982.

'The Government Inspector'

Aleksandrovsky, G. V. 'Этюды по психологии художественного творчества. «Ревизор» Гоголя, *Ежегодник коллегии П. Галачана*, 1898.
Belyayeva, L. A. 'К вопросу о положительном пафосе комедии Н. В. Гоголя «Ревизор»', *Ученые записки Московского областного пед. института им. Н. К. Крупской*, т.XVI, вып.4 (1958), 33–47.
Berkovsky, N. Ya. 'Комедия империи', in his *Литература и театр*, Moscow, 1969, 517–35.
Bertensson, S. 'The Première of "The Inspector General"', *Russian Review*, vii, I (1947), 88–95.
Bodin, P-A. 'The Silent Scene in Nikolaj Gogol's "The Inspector General"', *Scando-Slavica*, 33 (1987), 5–16.
Bogolepov, P. K. *Изучение комедии Гоголя «Ревизор»*. Moscow, 1958.
Börtnes, J. 'Gogol's "Revizor"—a Study in the Grotesque', *Scando-Slavica*, 15 (1969), 47–63.
Brodsky, N. L. 'Гоголь и «Ревизор»', in his *Н. В. Гоголь, «Ревизор»*, Moscow, 1927, V–LVII. Revised in his *Избранные труды*, Moscow, 1964, 40–84.
Brown, N. *Notes on Nikolai Gogol's 'The Government Inspector'*. Nairobi, 1974.
Bryantsev, A. A., Gippius, V. V. *et al. О «Ревизоре». Сборник статей*. Leningrad, 1936.
Burakovsky, S. Z. *«Ревизор» Н. В. Гоголя. 1836–1886 гг. Опыт разбора*. Novgorod, 1886.
Corbet, C. 'Le "Révizor" de Gogol devant la critique journalistique parisienne', *Revue de littérature comparée*, 33 (1959), 481–99.
Danilov, S. S. *«Ревизор» на сцене*. Kharkov, 1933. Revised ed., Leningrad, 1934.
Danilov, S. S. *«Ревизор» на Александринской сцене 1836–1936*. Leningrad, 1936.
Danilov, V. V. '«Ревизор» со стороны идеологии Гоголя', *Родной язык в школе*, 10 (1926), 13–21.
Debreczeny, P. 'The Government Inspector', in "Nikolay Gogol and his contemporary critics", *Transactions of the American Philosophical Society*, Vol. 56, Pt. 3 (1966), 17–29.
Degozhskaya, A. S., Chirkovskaya, T. V. *Комедия Гоголя «Ревизор»*. Leningrad, 1958.
Derzhavin, N. S. *Н. В. Гоголь: «Ревизор», комедия в 5 действиях. Сценическая история в иллюстративных материалах*. Moscow, 1936.
Dokusov, A. M., Marantsman, V. G. *Изучение комедии Н. В. Гоголя «Ревизор» в школе*. Moscow-Leningrad, 1967.
Dolgikh, A. I. 'К вопросу об индивидуализации и типизации речи персонажей. (Материалы сличения речи Городничего по трем редакциям комедии Н. В. Гоголя «Ревизор»)', *Русский язык в школе*, 2 (1959), 46–51.
Dolgikh, A. I. 'К вопросу об изобразительных возможностях синтаксиса русской разговорной речи. (Материалы сличения редакций комедии Н. В. Гоголя «Ревизор»)', *Ученые записки Орловского пед. института, кафедра русского языка*, т. 21, вып.6 (1962), 17–29.

Dolgikh, A. I. 'Типы диалога в комедии Н. В. Гоголя «Ревизор»', *Ученые записки Липецкого пед. института*, вып.3 (1963), 146-70.
Dolgikh, A. I. *Речевая характеристика персонажей в комедии Н. В. Гоголя «Ревизор».* (*При сопоставлении различных редакций произведения*). Abstract of dissertation. Moscow University, 1964.
Dolgikh, A. I. 'Структура диалога в комедии Н. В. Гоголя «Ревизор». (Средства связи реплик и их характерологические функции)', *Известия Воронежского государственного пед. института*, т.66 (1966), 5-22.
Dolinin, A. S. 'Из истории борьбы Гоголя и Белинского за идейность в литературе', *Ученые записки Ленинградского государственного пед. института*, т.XVIII, факультет языка и литературы, вып.5 (1956), 26-58.
Ehre, M. 'Laughing through the Apocalypse: The comic structure of Gogol's "Government Inspector"', *Russian Review*, 39 (1980), 137-49.
Eleonsky, S. F. 'Шесть редакций комедии Гоголя «Ревизор»', in his *Изучение творческой истории художественных произведений*, Moscow, 1962, 231-99.
Fedorenko, E. W. 'Gogol's "Revizor": A reexamination of language characteristics', *Russian Language Journal*, 106 (1976), 39-50.
Gerigk, H. J. 'Zwei Notizen zum "Revisor"', *Russian Literature*, IV/2 (1976), 167-74
Gippius, V. V. 'Работа Гоголя над образами «Ревизора»'. *Рабочий и театр*, 1 (1935), 20-2.
Gippius, V. V. 'Проблематика и композиция «Ревизора»', in *Н. В. Гоголь. Материалы и исследования*, Moscow-Leningrad, 1936, Vol. 2, 151-99. (English translation by R. A. Maguire in his *Gogol from the Twentieth Century*, Princeton, 1974, 216-65.)
Gippius, V. V. 'Заметки о Гоголе. III. Вариант Хлестакова', *Ученые записки Ленинградского университета, серия филологических наук*, т.76, вып.11 (1941), 9-12.
Gofman, V. A. 'Язык «Ревизора»', *Литературная учеба*, 6 (1934), 74-101.
Gofman, V. A. 'Язык и стиль «Ревизора»', in his *Язык литературы*, Leningrad, 1936, 301-38.
Grinkova, N. P. 'Из наблюдений над языком комедии Н. В. Гоголя «Ревизор»', *Русский язык в школе*, 2 (1952), 7-17.
Gukasova, A. G. 'Комедия «Ревизор». (Проблема типического в свете комедийного конфликта)', in *Гоголь в школе*, Moscow, 1954, 280-321.
Gurksy, V. K. *«Ревизор» Станиславского и... Гоголя*. Moscow, 1922.
Ivanov, V. V. '«Ревизор» Гоголя и комедия Аристофана', *Театральный Октябрь*, 1 (1926), 89-99. (English translation by R. A. Maguire in his *Gogol from the Twentieth Century*, Princeton, 1974, 200-14.)
Kas'yanov, A. V. 'Речевая характеристика персонажей комедии Н. В. Гоголя «Ревизор». (Из материалов наблюдений)', *Ученые записки Армавирского пед. института*, т.1 (1957), 57-109.
Kas'yanov, A. V. *Лексика и фразеология комедии Н. В. Гоголя «Ревизор»*. Dissertation. Московский государственный пед. институт им. В. И. Ленина, Moscow, 1958.
Kas'yanov, A. V. 'Лексика и фразеология комедии Н.В. Гоголя «Ревизор»', *Ученые записки Армавирского пед. института*, III/1 (1958), 183-230.
Kas'yanov, A. V. 'Особенности лексики и фразеологии комедии Н. В. Гоголя «Ревизор»', *Русский язык в школе*, 3 (1959), 20-7.
Kas'yanov, A. V. 'Речевые средства юмора и сатиры в комедии «Ревизор»', *Литература в школе*, 2 (1961), 58-61.
Kas'yanov, A. V. 'О речевых средствах юмора и сатиры в комедии Н. В. Гоголя «Ревизор»', *Ученые записки Армавирского пед. института*, т.4, вып.2 (1962), 3-19.
Kostelyanets, B. 'Еще раз о «Ревизоре»', *Вопросы литературы*, 1 (1973), 195-224.
Krestova, L. V. 'Зрители первых представлений «Ревизора»', *Научные труды Индустриально-педагогического института им. К. Либкнехта, серия социально-экономическая*, вып.8 (1929), 5-23.

Krestova, L. V. *Комментарий к комедии Н. В. Гоголя «Ревизор»*. Moscow, 1933.

Kupreyanova. E. N. 'Авторская «идея» и художественная структура «общественной комедии» Н. В. Гоголя «Ревизор»', *Русская литература*, 4 (1979), 3–16.

LeBlanc, R. D. 'Satisfying Khlestakov's appetite: The semiotics of eating in "The Inspector General"', *Slavic Review*, 47 (1988), 483–98.

Lotman, Yu. M. 'Историко-литературные заметки. 2. Городничий о просвещении', *Ученые записки Тартуского университета, литературоведение*, т.IX, вып.184 (1966), 138–41.

Lotman, Yu. M. 'О Хлестакове', *Труды по русской и славянской филологии*, Tartu, 26 (1975), 19–53. (English translation by R. Sobel in A. Shukman, *The Semiotics of Russian Culture*, Ann Arbor, 1984, 177–212.)

Maimin, E. A. 'Сюжетная композиция в драматическом произведении. Построение сюжета в комедии Гоголя «Ревизор»', in his *Опыты литературного анализа*, Moscow, 1972, 160–83.

Mann, Yu. V. *Комедия Гоголя «Ревизор»*. Moscow, 1966.

Mann. Yu. V. '«Ужас оковал всех...» (О немой сцене в «Ревизоре» Гоголя)', *Вопросы литературы*, 8 (1989), 223–35.

Nikolayev, D. P. 'Конфликт в комедии Гоголя «Ревизор»', in *Н. В. Гоголь. Сборник статей*, ed. by A. N. Sokolov. Moscow, 1954, 139–67.

Nordby, E. L. *Gogol's comic theory and practice in 'The Inspector General'*. Dissertation. Stanford University, 1971.

Pacini Savoj, L. 'Il "Revisore" e la "Follia Mistica" Gogoliana', *Ricerche slavistiche*, 1 (1952), 3–21.

Petrov. V. 'Пьеса и сценарий. К экранизации «Ревизора»', *Искусство кино*, 6 (1952), 108–17.

Pozdeyev, A. A. 'Несколько документальных данных к истории сюжета «Ревизора»', *Литературный архив*, Moscow-Leningrad, 1953, Vol. IV, 31–7.

Shenrok, V. I. 'Комедии Гоголя на сцене', in his *Материалы для биографии Гоголя*, Vol. 3, Moscow, 1895, 505–22.

Shklovsky, V. 'Ситуация, коллизия «Ревизора»', in his *Повести о прозе*, Moscow, 1966, Vol. 2, 112–22.

Smirnov, N. A. 'К литературной истории текста «Ревизора» Гоголя', *Известия Отделения русского языка и словесности АН*, т.6 кн.1 (1901), 235–41.

Smirnov, V. A. 'Комедия Н. В. Гоголя «Ревизор» как выдающийся памятник художественного слова. Опыт изучения средств речевой характеристики городничего и Хлестакова', *Ученые записки Горьковского пед. института*, т.17 (1955), 202–27.

Stender-Petersen, A. 'Gogol und Kotzebue. Zur thematischen Entstehung von Gogols "Revisor"'. *Zeitschrift für Slavische Philologie*, 12/1–2 (1935), 16–53.

Stepanov, N. L. 'Работа Н. В. Гоголя над языком «Ревизора»', *Театр*, 3 (1952), 28–40.

Stepanov, N. L. 'Сатира Гоголя на экране («Ревизор»)', *Искусство кино*, 1 (1953), 71–86.

Stolpyansky, P. 'Заметки на полях Гоголя. (Историко-библиогафические примечания)', *Ежегодник императорских театров*, VI (1910), 63–72.

Suprun. A. E. 'К характеристике языка «Ревизора»', in *Сборник научных работ студентов Киргизского университета*, вып.1, Frunze, 1954, 77–86.

Tabakov, O. 'A Soviet actor and director looks at Gogol and "The Government Inspector"', *Journal of Russian Studies*, 35 (1978), 24–8.

Tikhonravov, N. S. 'Первое представление «Ревизора» на московской сцене', *Русская мысль*, V (1886), 84–105.

Tikhonravov, N. S. 'Очерк истории текста комедии Гоголя «Ревизор»', in his *«Ревизор»*. *Первоначальный сценический текст*. Moscow, 1886.

Triomphe, R. 'Une comédie russe: le Révizor ou le jeu du rire et de la vertu', *Bulletin de la Faculté des Lettres de Strasbourg*, 33 (1954–55), 169–84.

Triomphe, R. 'Gogol und die russische Kritik über den *Revisor*', in *Vorträge auf den Berliner Slawistentagung*, Berlin, 1956, 140–61.
Tsitlevich, L. M. 'Сюжетно-композиционная система комедии Н. В. Гоголя «Ревизор»', *Вопросы русской литературы*, 55 (1990), 12–18.
Vishnevskaya, I. L. 'Что еще скрыто в «Ревизоре»?', *Театр*, 2 (1971), 92–104.
Voitolovskaya, E. L. *Комедия Н. В. Гоголя «Ревизор». Комментарий*. Leningrad, 1971.
Vorob'ev, P. G. 'Комедия «Ревизор» в практике изучения ее в средней школе', in *Изучение творчества Н. В. Гоголя в школе*, ed. by L. I. Timofeyev, N. V. Kolokol'tsev, Moscow, 1954, 61–90.
Wiens, H. *Die Geschichte einer Komödie. Die Entstehung von Gogols "Revisor". Seine Beurteilung durch die Zeitgenossen und die Reaktion des Verfassers*. Dissertation. Göttingen. 1946.
Wigzell, F. 'Gogol and Vaudeville', in *Nikolay Gogol: Text and Context*, ed. by J. Grayson and F. Wigzell. New York, 1989, 1–18.
Zelinsky, B. 'Gogol's "Revisor". Eine Tragödie?', *Zeitschrift für Slavische Philologie*, 36/1 (1971), 1–40.

English translations of *Ревизор*

Anderson, J. *The Inspector General. A satiric farce in three acts*. London & New York, 1931.
Campbell, D. J. *The Government Inspector*. London, 1947.
Cooper, J. *The Inspector*, in 'Four Russian Plays', London, 1972.
Dolman, J., Rothberg, B. *The Inspector-General (Revizór), a Russian farce-comedy*. Boston & Los Angeles, 1937.
Ehre, M., Gottschalk, F. *The Government Inspector*, in 'The Theater of Nikolay Gogol', Chicago U.P., 1980.
English, C., McDougall, G. *The Government Inspector*, in 'Nikolai Gogol. A Selection'. Moscow, 1980.
Garnett, C. *The Government Inspector*, in 'The Works of Nikolay Gogol', Vol. 6, London, 1926. Revised by L. J. Kent in 'The Collected Tales and Plays of Nikolai Gogol', New York, 1964.
Goodman, W. L. *The Government Inspector*. Adapted by H. S. Taylor. London, 1962.
Guerney, B. G. *The Inspector General*, in 'A Treasury of Russian Literature', New York, 1943.
Hart-Davies, T. *The Inspector. A comedy*. Calcutta, 1890.
Ignatieff, L. *The Government Inspector*. Adapted by P. Raby. Minnesota U.P., 1972.
MacAndrew, A. *The Inspector General*, in '19th Century Russian Drama', New York, 1963.
Magarshack, D. *The Government Inspector*, in 'The Storm and other Russian Plays', London, 1960.
Mandell, M. S. *Revizor, a comedy*. New Haven, 1908.
Marsh, E. O., Brooks, J. *The Government Inspector*. London, 1968.
Mitchell, A. *The Government Inspector*. (An adaptation). London & New York, 1985.
Reeve, F. D. *The Inspector General. A comedy in five acts*, in 'An Anthology of Russian Plays', Vol. 1. New York, 1961.
Saffron, R. *The Inspector General*, in 'Great Farces', London & New York, 1966.
Seltzer, T. *The Inspector-General; a comedy in five acts*. New York, 1916.
Seymour, J. L., Noyes, G. R. *The Inspector. A comedy in five acts*, in 'Masterpieces of the Russian Drama', London & New York, 1933.
Sykes, A. A. *The Inspector-General (or "Revizór")*. *A Russian Comedy*. London, 1892.

Index